GW01465420

Heartbeat Poetry

Amy Owens

Published in 2011 by New generation Publishing

Copyright © Text Amy Owens

First Edition

The author asserts the moral right under the Copyright, Designs and
Patents Act 1988 to be identified as the author of this work.

All Rights reserved. No part of this publication may be reproduced,
stored in a retrieval system or transmitted, in any form or by any means
without the prior consent of the author, nor be otherwise circulated in
any form of binding or cover other than that which it is published and
without a similar condition being imposed on the subsequent purchaser.

www.newgenerationpublishing.info

Contents

Blank pages at the back for notes

Introduction

I have always had a love of writing since I was a little girl never leaving home without a pen and piece of paper. Nowadays it's the click of the notes app on my I-phone as I find inspiration in random places at any given moment.

Life brings us many twists and turns and through many difficult times I have used writing as a way to find solace and hope. I want to use the poems I have written over the years to help others through their hard times and encourage people to put their trust in God. My prayer would be as you read these that you feel blessed, uplifted, encouraged, comforted, inspired and draw closer to God.

I would like to thank my husband, William, and my boys - Joshua, Matthew, Nathan and Joel for being patient and encouraging me on my journey and would like to dedicate this book in memory of my Mum and Dad - I love and miss you both.

Amy x

Discover the gift God has placed in your life then pursue it and live it with enthusiasm.

Check out Heartbeat Poetry on Facebook

Email: owensa79@gmail.com

Girly Gems

This chapter is a collection of poems specifically for girls - funny, serious, uplifting, encouraging. Hope you enjoy!

Rathfriland On The Hill

A little rugged town set on a hill
With the Mourne mountains as it's back drop
Beautifully sculpted with years of history
And the best ice cream sold in Grahams shop
Buildings so ancient although a little run down
full of character and stories untold
Add to the culture and familiarity
Of this wee town on the hill so old
Warm welcome for visitors as they pass through
Admiring the scenery as they stop for a rest
Helping us who live here to actually realise
In this wee town we are so blessed
Full of potential and talent
Even as you look at the building remains
It may be a small place compared to others
But it's amazing just what it contains
With years of memories recorded in print
From the amazing staff at the Outlook
This town is sure to leave lasting impressions
And secure a place in a history book
Let's enjoy and treasure our wee town
So those that follow us then always will
Be proud to embrace the history
And love living in Rathfriland On The Hill

Cottage Hideaway

Sometimes my days are crazy
Packed with so much to do
Remember this and pick up that
It's a struggle to see it through
It seems to spiral out of control
Like a whirlwind angry and strong
Building momentum and swirling round tasks
As time keeps ticking along
But then I stop and close my eyes
My shoulders drop to rest
As I picture my little hideaway
That secluded little cottage nest
There she sits hidden among the trees
Her beauty takes my breath away
Isolated yet she's not lonely
Enjoying each moment of the day
Put together from rough edged stones
Her outstanding frame beams with pride
And the little wooden swing in the garden
Is her constant companion close by her side
The lush green fields gently roll
As I watch from the country hedge
Sweeping carpets of colourful flowers
Down to the waters edge
Peacefully the water ripples
Like a gentle stirring of tea
As I draw In the smell of the summer
I think "this is the place for me"
The sun shines down upon me
And the soft breeze accompanies with a kiss
The birds serenade in harmony
As I think " where on earth could be better than this"
The smell from the cottage kitchen
Of fresh baked scones and apple pie
Fill the air with their tempting aroma
As the cool of the evening draws nigh
The table is lavished with good food
And buckets of chilled aged wine

Cottage Hideaway....... continued

As a log burns bright in the fire
And candles add a special touch ready to dine
I breath out with a feeling of satisfaction
A deep meaningful sigh
As I tell myself now I can open my eyes
To finish today's tasks I must try
And if and when it all gets too much
I can quiet myself until I hear my heart beat
And drift off again to my cottage hideaway
My safe haven - my summer retreat!

Halfway House

A little country cottage
Hidden somewhere no one sees
Nestled deep within the Mournes
Surrounded by tall trees
Gentle trickling water
Flows in the nearby stream
The table's set outside
With just baked scones and fresh whipped cream
The birds sing out in harmony
A sweet uplifting song
The world right now seems perfect
Nothing could be wrong
The rabbits bounce in nearby fields
Playing happily in the noon heat
While two friends enjoy a rest
In this their hideaway – their retreat
Forgetting all that bothers them
The pressures and the strife
Thinking of themselves for once
Not the chaos of family life
No worries about tomorrow
No thought or regret of the past
Just staying in the moment and hoping it will last
They both can sit in silence
And that's ok they don't mind
Two individuals with similar lives
They are one of a kind
So they can escape to their halfway house
When they need a quiet place as a crutch
When things build up and overwhelm
And all become too much
There they have each other
Someone to help and understand
A friend to dry away the tears
Just the way God planned
To laugh with in the good times
And encourage through the bad
We are the friends God put together
And of that I sure am glad

Come Rest

When you're tired and weary and your hearts feeling sore
And exhausted you think you simply can't take anymore
Then reach out to heaven God waits patiently
With arms outstretched He says "come give your burdens to Me"
You will find solace as you meet with Him there
Comfort and peace as you leave your worries and care
As you rest in His presence He will fill you with strength
Together you will be able to go any length
To power through life and be at your best
Then remember spend quiet time with God and simply rest

Simple Smiles

Often I smile when I watch my child play
Or grin when I hear what some people have to say
At times a clumsy moment turns to a smirk
When someone does something silly in the street or in work
Some days I watch my husband while he quietly sleeps
And I smile as I'm thankful knowing he is for keeps
Often I see people being just who they are
And teary eyed I proudly grin knowing they've come so far
Maybe these moments when I smile I should stop and glance
Hoping for eye contact just by chance
And share a little of my time with a simple smile
Showing that person they've made my day worthwhile

Creation Praise

Many days I've travelled these old familiar roads
Sat under the shade of the towering oak
Listened to the beautiful music of nature in harmony
Relaxed in the noonday sun, not a care in the world
I've climbed the mountains, struggling, pushing myself
To feel the satisfaction of accomplishment
I've mingled with creation and enjoyed partaking in her glory
But as I sit alone, listening to the summer rain
Weeping gently upon the canvas, falling like tears
Asking for my attention, I begin to realise
All long I have been looking but not seen
For as I quiet myself – my inmost thoughts
Not a care for tomorrow or question for now
I can suddenly see!
All of creation worships its Master
The trees sway gently in the soft, flowing breeze
Gracefully bowing in adoration
The flowers raise their heads towards heaven
In worship they offer what they have
Perfuming the air with praise
The mountains stand strong and courageous
Declaring Your majestic power and awesome glory
For all that You've made cry out in honour and majesty
Declaring You are Lord, Maker of Heaven and Earth
O Lord, may my eyes never again miss
The most beautiful and wonderful sight
Of Your creation
Giving all they have
Back to You in praise

The Battlefield

Sometimes my minds a battlefield
A bombardment like world war
Fighting, arguing, continual noise
I feel like diving to the floor
A constant tagging for my attention
I'm pulled in every way
I'd love to find a shelter
And momentarily hide away
Teen attitudes, children twisting
Babies piercing cry
Phone calls, questions, a list to do
Feels like bombs falling from the sky
And yet I wake each morning
And I'm thankful to face each day
As I think of that old battlefield
I know people are in a worse way
I may have wounds imprinted
And scars that never can be erased
But God still walks beside me
And upholds the family I have raised
So as a new day dawns
I look to God in prayer
For He's my shield and compass
Through good and bad He's always there

Hugs

Hugs are like a medicine
That have an instant healing effect
Whether you're feeling lonely or sad
Excited, happy or wrecked
They help relieve stress and tension
And they show other people you care
It's an excellent way without using words
To tell people if you need them you'll be there
So don't take a little hug for granted
It can mean more than you'll ever know
Why not just throw your arms round someone
And tell them that you love them so

Hug Someone

When you wrap your arms around someone
Watch their expression as you say
"Take a minute here with me
And tell me about your day"

Whether someone has a slow day
Or running at a frantic pace
You will never comprehend
How much they need a tight embrace

Sometimes words aren't needed
A simple smile will do
A hug and a smile are best friends
At telling someone "hey, I love you"

Tattered Heart

I saw a little tattered heart
With a colourful design
Decorated with strips of ribbon
And I thought 'that's just like mine'
It looked a little tender
Needing handled carefully
Then I heard God say 'that's what I do
When you give your heart to me.
I take the wounded and battered
Remnants of your heart
And I fix it gracefully together
So it won't fall apart
I weave colours into your life
Others will look and see
That even though the tough times come
I heal and restore so beautifully
When you feel that life has stripped you bare
And troubles never seem to cease
Just place your heart in my hands
I will transform it into an art piece'

Flower Garden

A flower garden would be quite boring
If they all looked the same
So too as flowers God has planted on earth
We are all different and when in bloom
We compliment each other
Don't strive to be a rose
If you are created a daffodil
Be the best you God has made you to be
Reach your full potential
Then synchronized with those around you
You will be part of an awesome display
Of beauty and majestic creation
It's better and more wonderful together

Blossom

A delicate little flower can blossom
In the hardest of places
So we too can beautifully blossom
No matter how difficult our surroundings
Or where we find ourselves
In fact doesn't a beautiful little flower
Blossoming somewhere where it shouldn't
Actually show Gods hand at work!
Don't despise where you are
At this moment as you don't know
What miracle you may be
To someone as they watch you
Flower in tough times

Open Up Little Bud

Oh little bud open up let your beauty show
Even though your gorgeous as a little bud yes I know
Raise that dropping head of yours and blossom into flower
Let the sunlight shine on you and be refreshed with a summer shower
Open up those petals stretch forth to heaven above
And everyone around you can then be touched with My love
You have been created with a purpose and a plan
Uniquely hand crafted - My design and sculpted by My hand
So be who I've made you to be please don't hide away
Others need to see you bloom remember I've made you this way

Jesus

Tell Me About Your Day!

Have you ever saw a father
Who has spent some time apart
From his little child
The centre of his heart
When they are reunited
The father on bended knee
Holds open wide his two arms
And beckons "come" so tenderly
With a smile as bright as sunshine
Eyes like an ocean that overflow
Love and passion overwhelming
Become a shining joyful glow
That's how Jesus welcomes us
Each and every day
Keen for us to spend time with Him
As He listens to what we have to say
He watches over us while we sleep
Waiting patiently for the dawn
Throughout the day He's by our side
Still there at our final yawn
Longing for time together
He calls out yearning just for me
To sit a while and talk with Him
And rest contentedly
No need for fancy conversation
I don't have to try and impress
No worries if I'm worn out
Or even if I look a mess
He wants me just to sit with him
To be myself and know all's ok
As he puts his arm around me and says
"Now tell me about your day!"

Patience

P ersevering under great pressure

A llowing God to refine you as treasure

T rusting in Him even under intense heat

I ndescribable peace knowing you wont be beat

E xcitedly waiting Gods answer to prayer

N eedless to say you'll know He'll be there

C ounting it all joy and facing life with calm

E xperiencing all things with the great 'I AM'

Amazing God

Wanna know one of the most wonderful things about God?
We can come to him without fear!
His mercy stretches out forgiveness when we do wrong
His grace covers us like a soft comforting blanket
When we are vulnerable
His love extends beyond what we can even imagine
Despite our ugliness
He loves us just the way we are
His tenderness touches our bruised wounds
Without hurting us in any way
His acceptance allows us to open up
Without any fear of rejection
His strength makes us strong
In our times of weakness
Filling us with supernatural courage
To face what comes our way
His understanding and compassion
Goes beyond what our human minds can conceive
Unlike anything else in life
He will never let us down
He is all we ever need
Our deepest yearnings cannot be satisfied without him
In other words
He is the great "I AM"

Don't miss the SONrise

(Isaiah 60)

As the sun bursts forth early in the morn
To announce the joy of a new day that is born
With it's vibrant fiery glow the world to adorn
Wake up! Don't miss the SONrise!

Its light radiates for everyone to see
And it's warmth a soothing comfort wherever you may be
Angels watch with anticipation of the jubilee
Wake up! Don't miss the SONrise!

Nothing can stop as it rises with power
Welcomed with grace by the opening petals of each flower
With rays of heat that pour down like a shower
Wake up! Don't miss the SONrise!

As the Son of God rises then wake up we must
He breaths into us life and we shake off the dust
Through his power we will shine with his glory as we trust
So wake up! Don't miss the SONrise!

In a world that is dark he has set us alight
People are drawn to such a wonderful sight
As we are called to arise, take our place with strength and might
Wake up! Don't miss the SONrise!

Don't slumber and sleep wasting time as you yawn
Moments will have passed and opportunities gone
Lift your face to the SON and others will be drawn
Wake up! Don't miss the SONrise!

Our light has come and we need to shine
Displaying to the world that Jesus is mine
How awesome and amazing is Gods wonderful design
So wake up! Don't miss the SONshine!

Count The Rainbows

When life brings a storm that sweeps you off your feet
And you're just rising up when you're knocked back and near beat
When you're gasping and ready to faint under intense heat
Don't count the storms count the rainbows!
Sometimes circumstances can rule how we feel
Overwhelmed we allow situations to steal
But to move on and be stronger so your heart can heal
Don't count the storms count the rainbows!
It's easy to complain and allow what's happening to dictate
With words like "another storm, typical that's great!"
Instead take a breath and tell your mind to 'wait'
And don't count the storms count the rainbows!
Often we cannot choose the storms coming our way
But if you hold on to Jesus then come what may
He'll anchor you deep you won't be swept away
If you don't count the storms count the rainbows!
So think about the outlook you have in running this race
And remember it doesn't matter what storm you face
A rainbow will appear - Gods smile of grace
Just don't count the storms count the rainbows!

Unlock And Download

How many times do we hide away
Keeping how we feel under disguise
Thinking if we can just smile and pretend
People won't know "I'm fine" is actually lies
So often we hold on to what we go through
Stored away under lock and key
Thinking it's not safe to allow others in
Feeling vulnerable to what people may see
Yet what we don't realise if we'd just open up
A world of opportunity appears
To share golden nuggets of experience
That can bring peace to other people's fears
God cannot pour in to a tightly closed vessel
It takes more than to simply believe
God has an abundance to give us
If we open up our hearts to receive
So loosen the vice grip, relax just a little
Change out of the " closed up" mode
Tune into Gods presence and allow others to help
Its time to unlock and download!

Love

A helping hand to do a chore
A loving kiss on a little childs sore
The extra mile when you want to do no more
Love!
The greeting at the door with a happy smile
The "let's have coffee and chat a while"
That arm round someone saying "you're worthwhile"
Love!
Making the effort to say "well done"
Spending time with a child to just have fun
Thinking less of "me" and more of "someone"
Love! love! love!

What Is Love?

That fast beating heart when he looks your way
Or your blushing cheeks with every word he may say
Your wandering mind cannot concentrate
Or hours of preparing before a date
WHAT IS LOVE?
Is it a lifetime of commitment not only romance
Growing old together not just a fleeting glance
United experiencing life cruel and kind
Still standing as one both hearts entwined
WHAT IS LOVE?
Or the cry of a newborn you have carried within
As they lay in your arms and you touch their soft skin
The joy of a toddler as they achieve so much for the first time
Their first words, first steps or reciting a rhyme
WHAT IS LOVE?
Maybe it's the time as you watch the kids go
Love is now learning to release and let go
No more a child a young adult looks at you
As you contemplate the happy years and how they have flew
WHAT IS LOVE?
Sometimes it's the moment when you loose someone dear
And realise how much they mean to you with each falling tear
That overwhelming emotion of just one more day
As you think back of everything they used to do and would say
WHAT IS LOVE?
Maybe its that closeness between honest good friends
A chance to be real no more need to pretend
Knowing I'm my sisters keeper and act like I should
That safe healing haven just like at sisterhood
WHAT IS LOVE?
Love can be explained differently by everyone
Experiences in life what you've been through and done
Yet one thing unites us we can feel deep true love
Unconditional and forgiving and comes from heaven above
Laying down a life greater love has no man that this
That's heaven embrace and the Fathers kiss
THAT IS LOVE!
And now these three remain: faith, hope and love, but the greatest of these is love.
1 Corinthians 13

Wasted Years

I woke up this mornin and rolled outa bed
Tuttin i thought "ack I've a sore head"
Stumbling to the bathroom I washed the sleep from my eyes
I glanced in the mirror and thought "whow how time flies"
My face was much fuller and skin not just as tight
My eyelids were droopin and I thought "this cant be right"
I rushed through the mornin with all the usual chores
Dustin and ironin and washin the floors
But in the back of my mind mingled with worries and fears
Was a woodpecker tappin "wasted years wasted years"
So I got to a thinkin with a deep heavy sigh
Ive go to do something to live before I die
No more waitin or wonderin excuses must go
Ive got to allow what's within me to flow
No more wasting time thinkin what could have been
When there's so much within that people haven't yet seen
So I've come to realise before the final rapture
There are millions of moments I can ignore or can capture
I can use what I have and give of my best
Hey who even knows how many people could be blessed

Woven Tapestry

One day I went to visit Grandma
And there upon her knee
Where lots of different threads
As she began her tapestry
I watched her weave intently
Knowing exactly what to do
Knotting the different colours
New patterns coming through
I couldn't see what she saw
For she had a picture in her mind
The difficulties didn't bother her
There was no fussing of a kind
It didn't seem that great at first
As I watched her from the door
The knots looked out of place
Until I observed her do some more
Each time I went to visit
Her hands moved swiftly with no fear
I marvelled how it started out
And now an artwork did appear
Then I heard God speak to me
He said "now do you understand
I take your wounds and heartache
And weave them gently in My hand
The trials that you go through
When you think that life's unfair
Remember what I thread together
Will be something you can share
The pain and suffering you go through
In you I work it beautifully
I see the bigger picture
Your life's a tapestry

A String To The Bow

I argued with God one day
That life just didn't seem fair
Saying " I'm going through so much
And I don't even think that You care
Bad things are constantly happening
And I haven't got any control
If I just had a little reprieve
Then I would be on a roll
But I seem to be just like a punch bag
That always is getting knocked down
Whenever I squeeze out a grin
It's not long before it turns to a frown
Could You tell me what is the meaning
To this heartache and these constant tests
I thought whenever I followed You
My life would surely be blessed"
Then I went and sat in the corner
With a moan and a deep heavy sigh
My eyes were so swollen and tired
They no longer were even fit to cry
When oh so softly and gently
I heard God speak to my heart
"Oh my wonderful, precious child
I've been with you right from the start"
I looked but I couldn't see Him
But I felt His warm tender smile
Whispering so lovingly in my ear
"Wait and see it will all be worthwhile"
My mind was so anxious and restless
I couldn't see and I couldn't understand
But He quietly reminded me again
"My child I have your life all planned
Through you I have chosen to minister
To the hurting the sad and the lost
Many will come to you heartbroken
Many who have counted the cost
As you sit with them and listen
Tears of healing and release will then flow
Cause each hard time you've been through in life

A String To The Bow....... continued

Is another string to your bow
Life does have difficulties and trials
But don't worry come as they may
With My love and sufficient grace
It will allow you more music to play
So don't be disheartened and discouraged
With the many obstacles that you may face
They are laying the pathway to others
For you to share My love and grace"

Hope

At times life's problems can press hard upon us
We become exhausted with stress
Yet no matter how difficult things become
There is always hope
When we hope we become strengthened within
It tells us never to give in
Hope will become a light when all around is darkness
When everything seems bleak and useless
Hope will never say give up
Hope when hand in hand with faith is mighty
Faith will take our wore out wings
And cause us to soar high in the sky like an eagle
Hope will lift you above life's situations
But faith will move you over them
Faith is the wind beneath the wings of hope

Girls

G od made us special and unique

I ntricately designed with a purpose

R eaching where no man can reach

L oving beyond our understanding

S haring the fathers heart as He designed

Woman

W onderfully created by the Masters hand

O utstandingly gifted and talented

M ultitasker what more can I say

A mazing overcomer

N urturing heart of God

God's Girl

She awakes in the morning to a day
Filled with opportunities not fear
The first words to leave her lips are
"Morning Father God"
She looks in the mirror and remembers
No matter what the reflection shows
She is a strong overcoming woman
Placed here with a purpose
Equipped for the job in hand
Nothing can separate her from Gods love
As she faces her day she realises
Those hurdles are simply exercises
Stretching her faith
And helping her reach her full potential
She is the daughter of the Most High King
A princess and a ray of Gods glory
Shining forth an awesome display of grace
Her faith collides with Gods purpose
And explodes with an array of colour
Touching the lives of those that come across her path
She knows she serves an all powerful God
And that nothing is impossible.
Through Him she can do all things
And will strive to inspire and encourage others to believe!
She understands the need and power
Of coming together in unity
With other like minded girls
She's certain "it's better together"
As she lays her head down at night peace is her friend
As she places her trust in God she can rely on him and REST

R eassuring
E verlasting
S teadfast
T rust

Precious Princess

Oh My precious princess
How I love to spend this time with you
As you walk slowly along the carpet of gold
Thinking how much you enjoy
Feeling the sand between your toes
I smile as I watch you marvel at the tiny grains
They sparkle like diamonds in the sun
They glitter upon your face like jewels
And reflect your beauty back to Me
I am glad that you are Mine
I tell the sun to come comfort you
To warm you so you relax
Then I whisper in a gentle breeze
As I brush your hair from your face
I LOVE YOU, I LOVE YOU, I LOVE YOU
As you gaze out towards the ocean
I can hear the millions of thoughts
Running wildly through your mind
So I crash the waves
Loudly against the rock face
So I may have your attention
The water gleams with delight
It shimmers and shines
Dancing and swaying
Celebrating how much
I long for us to be together
Yes, you can see the beauty that surrounds
The wonderful things that I have created
But in the midst of this picture perfect moment
The beauty I see radiates from you
I long for these little pauses in time
When you truly see how much you mean to Me
For I delight in you
I romance you in uncountable ways
But it is only a few precious moments
When you hear how I feel
For you tend to think why

Precious Princess........continued

Why would I your Creator and Saviour
Want to romance you?
Well it's because I love you
With an everlasting love
A love no human mind can conceive
And I will continue
To tell you over and over again
You are beautiful!
You are precious!
You are Mine!

Your Father

Sisterhood - Girls Together

Tall and strong and proud she stands
A purpose to achieve
United with her sisters
Such power when they believe
Different women join together
Many simply becoming one
Declaring freedom, breaking chains
Worshipping Gods only son
Arrayed with mercy, etched with beauty
Compassion highlights her smiling face
An outstretched hand of kindness
A strong yet gentle display of grace
She raises up those who have fallen
And strengthens the feeble and the weak
Watching over all her sisters
She's the voice for those who cannot speak
With courage she will go beyond
Stepping out of her comfort zone
With tender arms and tears of compassion
She befriends those who are alone
Uplifting others with encouragement
No matter what she will be there
With shoulders strong enough to lean on
She carries her sisters on the wings of a prayer
The Fathers heart she wears like a necklace
Displayed for all the world to see
Standing proud daughters of the king
They know it's better together in unity
Supporting and loving one another
Just the way they know they should
Rejoicing together whoop de whoop
One love, One heart, One sisterhood!!

Add Colour

Bring out all those lovely ladies
All colours, shapes and sizes
Who will go the distance for Jesus
No turning back or compromises
Let us stand together
And hold each others hand
Discovering with excitement
The great things that God has planned
Upholding one another
Supporting each others dreams
Helping those we meet on our journey
To take heart no matter how difficult it seems
Let's add a splash of colour
To the lives of those along the way
A kind word, a smile, a cuppa
It can simply make someone's day
Lets remember each and every girl
Has a unique purpose and design
That God has put within us gifts
Yours may differ from mine
But that's what makes it special
When we come together with one mind
God adds "super" to our natural
All things become possible we find
So let's join with all our sisters
And be amazed what God can do
Simply by allowing Him
To work through me and you

A Woman's Work Is Never Done!

Dirty dishes, dried out hands
A hot and sweaty brow
Beds to fix, clothes to fold
The kids will be coming home now
Hoover out, pets to feed
Grocery shopping somewhere in between
Face to tidy and hair to brush
Well in this state I just can't be seen
Floors to mop, furniture to dust
Bathroom needs attention it's in a state
Finish it later, collect the kids
Then appointments – cannot be late
Schedules, homework, ironing to do
Ingredients out I promised I'd bake
All measured and organised
But first the dinner to make
Hubby home as you take a breath
With a smile and a how was your day
Tick list running through your mind
As you tell yourself I can handle what comes my way
Kids all bathed and story read
Kisses and time to rest
When a little voices echo's in the dark
Mummy I love you - you're the best
Lunches made and diary out
Tomorrow all sorted and planned
When your phone unexpectedly beeps
A girl friend – she will understand
A brief few words of encouragement
And a smile decorates the heart
We all know that every home
Without a woman would fall apart
She can accomplish such a hectic day
And still find some time for fun
Simply because she's a woman
And a woman's work is never done!

Amazing Woman

A gentle and quiet nature
Always willing to help and to share
Such qualities to find in one person
Are both outstanding and rare
You have taught me so much already
By how you handle what comes your way
With such kindness and soft spoken words
That help so many people day after day
I stand in awe at your calmness
Despite the mountain of pressure you face
Going beyond the call of duty
With eloquence, meekness and grace
I hope one day that by watching you
That I can somehow learn to share
A little piece of your nature
And the magnificent way that you care
Money nor experience can't achieve what you possess
I hope you come to realise
How many lives you touch and bless

Detailed

She wakes in the morning and has a shower
Powdered and pampered - going well so far
Clothes picked out with shoes to match
Deodorant in handbag incase of a damp patch
Nails all painted and of course the toes
Extra things packed incase a flaw shows
Make up applied now hair to groom
So much time spend on detail before she leaves the room
Accessories in place she again turns back
Another look in the mirror one final check
Then she leaves happy and content
Knowing she is her best with the time she spent
Isn't it amazing how she doesn't seem to understand
The detail God went to when crafting her with His hand
Such attention paid He sculpted her til 'just right'
He smiled knowing she was perfect in his sight
Now as she gets ready applying her face
She can think of the detail God went to sculpting her by His grace

Busy Modern Woman

Life is so busy she doesn't know how she copes
It even requires watching sky plus to see the soaps
Frantically running the kids everywhere
While trying to schedule an appointment for hair
Has to apply make up mmm what colours to choose
Making sure they match the outfit and of course the shoes
Then let the day begin there are groceries to buy
Trolleys crashing together with a dirty look and and a sigh
Buy it all in one shop don't worry bout the price
Then thinks " I need some cake and not just one slice
Will exercise later to work off the cals
Then must arrange a time to meet up with the pals"
As she dashes around the pensioner in front
Becomes an irritation as she pushes past with a grunt
Then back to the car at a frantic pace
As she babbles giving off saying "is this a snails race"
Her mind in a spin as she thinks what needs done next
Have to sort dinner and the dishwasher needs fixed
Washing and ironing and dusting to do
She can catch her breath for two minutes if she nips to the loo
Now to pick the kids up with homework to complete
Not a moment to rest she is feeling totally beat
But must go on still have so much to achieve
If throwing in a quick prayer for strength she wonders will she receive
Then dinner and washing up and lunches to make
Preparing for the next day she's thinking "where did today go goodness sake"
Eventually kids to bed she lies in a heap
While hubby interestedly inquires "are the kids all asleep"
She battles a moment wondering 'is my head sore'
Feeling tired she tells herself "keep going just a little while more"
She agonizes over eating too much she needs to get fitter
While she logs on to Facebook and checks out twitter
While everyone talks bout how wonderful life is
She wonders why her day seems to have her in a tizz
Then lights out for everyone she exhaustedly lies
Amazed how she couldn't fit more in today - time flies
Her body is weak but her eyelids won't close
As motionless in the dark silence she plans her tomorrows

Busy Modern Woman.......continued

With a quick little thought just before she goes to sleep
She mutters "God help me tomorrow my schedule to keep
Give me extra hours or freeze time better still
So I can accomplish all I can and your will
I promise I'll spend more time with you and to pray
I just need more hours to fit into my day"
Then God gently whispers as he breaths upon her goodnight
Slow down my precious and you'll be alright
It's moments with Me that will fuel your strength
As we spend time together you'll find you can go any length
If you take a few moments to stop you'll realise
You're squeezing too much in your day - you need to prioritise
Just rest in my presence in my tender care
And when you wake in the morning I'll still be there

Who Is The Virtuous Woman

Who is this virtuous woman that the bible holds in high esteem
The one that cause most women to shake in fear it would seem
Maybe if we take a look at her then we may even find
That we're really not that different and not that far behind
She cooks and cleans for her family preparing all the meals
She dries the tears of her children we know exactly how that feels
Working hard she provides their clothes she may knit and darn
But we know how tiring it is to stand for hours at the iron
With the children taken care of her attention turns to her home
Who can relate to going through the house with a fine brush comb
She sweeps and organizes keeping everything in it's place
And after she has that complete she tidies up her face
Her husband arrives home she looks her best and with a smile and a
hmmm
She forgets all else around her and devotes her time to him
She'll meet his every need and not just as it is her duty
Its because she loves her husband and that is her inner beauty
In Proverbs 31 she may not have had all that much
But we can see what she can achieve with the Masters touch
Today we may be busy with a crazy and hectic lifestyle
But when we devote ourselves to Jesus He'll show us how to make life
worthwhile
Even nowadays your life may be nothing at all like mine
But with Jesus as our focus He'll cause that inner beauty to shine
So I don't think we need to fear our wonderful virtuous friend
I reckon we have a lot in common we may just be a different blend
So don't be too hard on you and give yourself a little credit
The closer we walk with Jesus He will show us what we need to edit
So let us walk with confidence with Jesus hand in hand
Uplifting one another and fulfilling what he has planned

From STRESSED to BLESSED

S tart taking care of yourself
T rust and commit your ways to God
R ealise God loves you unconditionally
E xercise to clear your head
S alvage a little "me time"
S treamline a hectic schedule
E njoy moments with good friends
D iscipline yourself to time with God

T ackle problems head on - don't worry
O n the odd occasion have a duvet day!

B elieve what Gods word says about you
L ean on a carefully chosen few for support
E nergise your day by starting it with God
S trive to reach your full potential
S tep up to new challenges
E ncourage and build up yourself and those around you
D esire and pursue Gods will for your life

A Woman of Strength

How can we start to understand
What makes a woman strong
Her enduring fight and courage
When all around her things things go wrong
What gives her that unending strength
To face yet another day
In the midst of raging storms
She can still stand come what may
Where does she find that warming smile
When situations all go wrong
Or in those trying sad times
Still can sing a song
Where does she find the energy
To accomplish all she has to do
And still hold on to patience
To help others in need too
The secret to a woman's strength
It simply must be stated
Is all in her design
And the way she was created
For God smiled when he made a woman
He stood back and said "that's good
I've created a masterpiece
That can share my heart like no other could"

Heavens Tea Party

I watch the little faces
As they gratefully enjoy a feed
So many men, women and children
Hungry and in need
And yet they keep on smiling
Despite the little they possess
They don't care about fancy things
Or try hard to impress
In my mind it seems so unfair
How the world is ill divided
So sad to watch people suffering
So now I have decided
That one day when God calls us home
We will in unison be hearty
And with the prettiest cups and saucers
We will join together for 'Heavens tea party'
Sparkles, flowers, teapots too
All colours, shapes and sizes
An open invitation
Where no one worries or compromises
Everyone welcome no difference made
Music accompanied by peaceful trust
Ribbons and napkins and places set
Sprinkled with love and star dust
What an image I hold in my thoughts
When we all become one and we sing
Joining the party in heaven
Praising Jesus our King!

This is for my friend Leeanne who makes beautiful creations to raise money to help others.

BittyButton

She works so hard in her little house
Making peoples treasures
Cutting, sticking, ruling
Singing as she measures
With an open house invitation
She sets people's hearts aglow
As they arrive to ponder over gems
They see an explosion of colours like a rainbow
Sewing machine at the ready
Paper, felt and glue
Handcrafted little ponders
Made with BittyButton love just for you
Adding that special personal touch
That makes each item so unique
Loud and clear the message is heard
Without ever having to speak
Somewhere in each creation
You will find a button - her signature mark
Making smile all who purchase
Bringing an extra spark
So check out BittyButton
And each heaven made little gift
Comes with a warning though you've been told
"These items encourage, inspire and uplift"

This was written for my friend Laura who makes beautiful little button creations.

Random

This section contains a mixture of poems from friends to simple smiles. Enjoy having a read and hopefully a smile.

My Friend

God looked down and smiled one day
And said I'll give this world a treasure
Someone that will show My love
In a way no one can measure
I'll bless her with kindness and gentleness
And overflow her with My love from the start
I will pour out My gracefulness upon her
So through her I can touch people's hearts
I will adorn her with mercy and faithfulness
And her smile with be as warm as the sun
And through this dear life I'll be glorified
A great work through her will be done
I'll clothe her with patience and endurance
Loving kindness will extend from her hand
I will place deep within her a pure heart
And listening ears to help and understand
She will be a blessing to others
A friend so unique and special to find
All who know her will love and respect her, a gem so valued and kind
Her heart will be trusting and compassionate
Wisdom will follow her all her days
Blessed will be all who befriend her
For once a friend she's a friend always
For sometimes I need angels upon earth
To help those who may be in need
That's why I will place her among you
For she sure is an angel indeed!
For when I planned and made her
The mould was broken so handle with care
She's My priceless gift and My jewel
Too wonderful for Me not to share
May she realise the wealth of her value
Rich with goodness and mercy and love
For just as each person on earth does
I smile when I look at her from above
For you are special beyond words
Though you probably can't comprehend
Just simply how much you are adored
By all of your family and friends

Nanny and Granda

I'm not a sentimental person
My emotions are difficult to express
But I just want to tell you both
It doesn't mean I love you any less
You have been so good to me
In every way throughout my life
Always there to stand up for me
And even help when I'm in strife
I know that I can turn to you
No matter if things are tough
You'll never turn me away
Or say right that's enough
So Nanny and Granda
I just want to say
Thanks and I love you
Both more every day

First Day at Playschool

I watched as he got out of bed
So excited he was shaking
I smiled and acted just like him
Though inside I was quaking
Breakfast gobbled up in a hurry
As I encouraged him to sit
Trying to delay the uniform
Just another little bit
'I need my bag and I need my clothes'
Is all that he could say
'Hurry mummy quickly
I'm going to playschool today'
I looked at him standing all so proud
In the clothes so fresh and new
As tears begin to wash my face
And I say 'Ahh I'm gonna miss you!'
How did this happen I ask myself
As we stand waiting in the hall
Time has gone so quickly
I still think that he's too small
At last the school door opens
He enters quietly standing at the back
I explain yet again about the toilet, the teacher and the snack
I tell him with a kiss I will collect him soon
He says 'I'm a big boy now I'm three'
As I tearfully leave him behind
He shouts out 'Hey I love you Mummy'
I know it's all part of growing up
It's just something that they do
But for a Mummy leaving a little child
It's a painful experience to go through
So we are all in this together Mums
We know how to sympathise
When we see another mum
As she stands at the school gate and cries

Compassion

Little tear filled eyes that weep
So silent and so still
Lonely and afraid
And with bellies they can't fill
Watching parents being killed
Living life in fear
Wishing someone would shelter them
Someone to draw near
No one in their world that cares
As they think what is my life about
All they need is love and a little help
Someone to reach out
They don't care about new gadgets
Or desire to have the latest fashion
Can you be the difference
And work alongside 'compassion'
Together we can be the voice
For those that can't be heard
All that we possess in life
Is more enjoyable when it's shared
Take a step reach out a hand
A little can mean a lot
Show the people around the world
That they haven't been forgot

We have all seen the little faces of children that are helped by Compassion. Reach out and help a little child.

I'm Nearly Here Mama

Mama you have helped me grow inside here I'm safe and warm
You have done your very best to protect me from any harm
I love to quietly listen to the sound of your heartbeat
Can you feel me poking you with my tiny hands and feet?
I stretch and yawn and move around but I'm running out of space
And I'm really looking forward to your kiss upon my face
I want to lie close in your arms and watch you as you smile
And I haven't long to wait now I'll be here in just a little while
I know your voice already I can hear you talk to me
And I'm glad that you're my Mummy we match each other perfectly
God said that you can borrow me and then you will understand
How it feels to hold a piece of heaven tenderly in your hand
So just you rest a little longer very soon my face you'll see
I really love my Mama and I know that she loves me!

The Abandoned Ship

She sits so lonely upon the stones
Abandoned and neglected
Gazing out across the sea
Where once her beauty was reflected
She watches with a saddened stare
Tears have left their rusting mark
As she recalls each story
And the journey she did embark
Her frame still stands so proud and tall
Her dignity still intact
She just needs a little love
Some kindness and respect
Her paintwork crumbles her body rots
Seagulls perch upon her towering mast
As she looks out upon her home
And thinks of her life gone past

My Son I Will...

I will love you I promise until eternity ends
Shelter you no matter what storm life sends
I will protect you forever until the day I die
Laugh with you and dry your tears when you cry
I will spend time chatting to hear your voice
Not because I have to but because that's my choice
I will hug you when you feel isolated and alone
I will quietly listen when you need to moan
I will encourage and tell you that you CAN achieve
I will pray with you and stand with you to believe
I will cheer you on in everything telling you not to hide
I will shelter you as I walk by your side
I will cheerfully declare to the world aloud
That I am you mum and of that I'm so proud
I will tell you daily your amazing simply because its true
Nothing or no one can change my love for you
So hold your head high believe and walk tall
You were made to be you - no one else at all
So in those dark moments when your quiet and still
Remember my son I love you and I will....

For Joshua, Matthew, Nathan and Joel. I love you all and forever I will...

Midnight Hour

Quietly she sits in the midnight hour
Her weary head resting in her hand
A portrait of silence and peacefulness
Yet a closer look reveals her mind is a raging storm
Gathering strength and momentum
With every unanswered question and thought
A whirlwind violently flows through her
Although it has not portrayed itself in her outward appearance
Motionless – yet she holds her frame with strength and endurance
Her eyes are empty and distant
Like a sailor lost at sea
They cry out but are not heard
Her eyelids barely flicker
Except to try and catch the fallen tear
That now escapes in her moment of vulnerability
With a huge gasp she inhales
As if she had been under water for this journey
Her eyes blinking twice as fast
And her heart pumping with a sudden rush of adrenalin
She raises her head and stands to her feet
Where she will now join the rest of the world
In the remaining hours of rest
No one will know, no one will have seen
Her momentary lapse of strength
Her soul exposed for a brief moment
She will sleep, waken and start again
Until her next midnight hour

Sea

Back and forth a rhythmic sound
A melody unique played in harmony with nature
A symphony of majestic creation
Orchestrated by the masters hand
Piano - the waves lap gently to the sandy beach
Then as if telling a story the intensity builds
Until forte - wave after wave crash loudly upon the shore
Backed by the whistling of the mighty wind
As it picks up golden grains of sand
And they dance in a frenzy
Twirling and swirling as if happy to be united
Then slowly the wind tires and comes to rest
Placing the millions of crushed sparkles gently back where they belong
With a soothing lullaby the wind says goodbye
And earth is cradled goodnight
With the rocking of the tender sea
The sound of the ocean waves

The Sailor And The Ship

He stands upon the oceans edge
Silver haired with matching beard
Much like the abandoned ship
Weather beaten and battle scars showing
He looks out into the vast blue space
And I wonder....
As the cold waves gently lap
Upon the ships hull
Tempting and teasing her
Back to where she once belonged
Her rusting frame now weakened
Slumps into the damp dark sand
Still he stares into the horizon
Side by side they silently recall
Centuries of years together
Out in the wide open sea
No thought for today and no care for tomorrow
Little did they know then
That today would come
And all those times
Would become a scrapbook of memories
That together they would share
A private collection
Now anchored upon the shore
As the ocean is called back
Away from land
The icy trickle flows over his toes
Drips fall from the her towering frame
As if in mourning
And he turns to her with tear filled eyes
"Fair well my friend alas our journey is complete"

I wrote this while sitting on a large stone on Cranfield beach while the sun was going down watching an old man look out into the vast ocean and I couldn't help but wonder..

Windy Day

The cotton wool clouds move swiftly by
As if in a race through the powder blue sky
The trees dance in a frenzy side by side
While the leaves madly scurry around and collide
The wind whistles loudly it's own version of a song
Inviting all it comes in contact with to join along
People, head down, using their hands as a shield
Hair blown in all directions like the grass in the field
So if you venture out in the wind for a stroll
May it be a powerful reminder that Gods in control

Reflection

As I sit here upon this rock
By the edge of the rippling water
Watching the fish make patterns
As they leap into the air
My thoughts focus on heaven
How in all this vast beauty
Does he take notice of me?
The mountains stretch into the sky
Covered in an array of colours
Each towering tree a different shade
The summer sun glistens upon the still waters
Sparkling like a sea of diamonds
The birds sing in harmony like a church choir
Each chirp a distinguished pitch of its own
A sound no man could re create
The gentle breeze blows softly through the trees
Like a whisper from above
The leaves shiver and shake
Dancing and celebrating a new day
The powder blue sky with its cotton wool clouds
Captivate me – a whole new world
Lie beyond its covering
The sweet aroma of wild flourishing flowers
Perfume the air with a smile
Like all of creation at this moment
They worship the One who made them
Thank you Lord and Savour
That as small and insignificant as I seem at this moment
You look from heaven and smile on me
You know my thought from afar
Your presence surrounds me like the air I breath
May I always keep this moment of awe and wonder
At the centre of my heart

Whispering Wonderland

Stepping out onto the frosty ground
The chilly night air almost takes my breath away
Snow covers the garden like a soft woollen blanket
Topped with millions of crushed diamonds
Scattered like sand across a beach
The rooftops glisten with a fine dusting
Like icing sugar beaten through a sieve
The cloudless dark blue sky with its bright shining moon
Light up the winter wonderland
With a strange bluish tint
Like looking through faint coloured glass
No movement no sound all is still
The weather beaten hedge stands tall and proud
That it has fought and overcome the bitter elements
Decorated with a thick white coat
Faraway fields almost come alive
With the radiance of the beauty of their top skin
Distant mountains highlight the horizon
With their thick snow capped peaks
That seem to drizzle to the bottom
Like a heavy topped melting ice-cream
Inviting, alluring, cold
Still – all is silent
As my body shivers and the icy breeze nips at my nose I realise..
Another year has gone
A new one has arrived just within seconds

Frosty Morning Rainbow

I awaken to a frozen world
Icy paths glitter and dance
Delighted to once again be set free
To display to all of nature their beauty
Cautiously I set out
Onto the slippery slide
Begging the elements to be kind
Convincing myself and the ice
That I am a friend
The dark night sky brightens
Shades of watery blue
Mixed with grey
And hints of pink
A beautiful artistic design.
Behind me the sun rises from its slumber
Almost burning the sky
With its fiery red glow
Displaying its mighty power
As it stretches forth
Bringing a new day
The frozen trees slowly weep
With the radiating heat from the sun
As I gaze upwards to the paint palate
In the sky above
I see it – curving and reaching
As if to envelope me
THE BRUSH STROKE OF PROMISE!
Multicoloured, illuminating
Although no words appear
They flash through my mind
As quick as lightening
Causing my heart to skip a beat
HOPE, FAITH, LOVE!

Mystery Morning

It's a strange morning
I scurry to the car
And quickly jump in
Trying to avoid the bitter cold air
I fumble with the keys
And it takes numerous attempts
To start the engine
Reluctantly I take hold of the steering wheel
My hands so cold they no longer hurt
My journey begins
The thick dense fog creeps eerily
Through the frozen trees
Enveloping everything in my view
Creating an illusion
That I have been transported
Into a faraway magical land
Where all is covered over
With a blanket of white
Highlighted with shades of black and grey
Anxiety grips me as the car slides
Like an ice skate across a frozen lake
So little control makes my body seize
Fear and excitement almost makes my beating heart stop
As they are shaken together inside me
Like a swirling snow globe
The hedges and trees stand still
Icicles decorate them
Covering them completely
Not a sound not a movement
I stop the car and cautiously step out
Being careful not to stumble
The freezing fog makes me gasp
As I breath out
The heat from my body
Reacts with the chilly air
And creates a string of steam
Which quickly disappears
Into the white winter wonderland
As I look towards what should be the town

Mystery Morning.......continued

All I see is hundreds of blurry lights
Swooping and dodging in every direction
They look like dancing fireflies in a frenzy
I pause for a moment
To appreciate and drink in
That here I am standing
Facing one of the most majestic scenes
That may ever be
I don't want to rush
Afraid that I may miss something amazing
Then – with a deep breath
I turn and walk towards work
Where my normal day begins
Will my magical scene
Still be there to transport me home?

Little Ponders

This section is just shorter quotes - just a little thought to ponder over in your mind throughout the day and maybe share with others.

Being a strong woman does not mean you don't feel weak - it means
despite the weakness you carry on

----------x----------

Strength, endurance,courage
Are more essential to a woman
Than the essentials her handbag contains

----------x----------

Makeup can cover flaws and imperfections
But Gods grace and forgiveness
Does not cover up
It removes our sins

----------x----------

It's when you are about to give up that a miracle shows up. Gods timing
is perfect

----------x----------

I am sisterhood
When you fall I will pick you up
When you cry I will dry your tears
When you laugh I will rejoice with you
For I am my sisters keeper

Girls may sparkle and glitter
Like jewels in a crown
But together they are courageous
And can turn the world upside down

----------x----------

When you look into the mirror remember that your heavenly Father
says:
You are beautiful!
You are precious!
You are mine!

----------x----------

When you look in the mirror
I want you to see
How beautiful, how wonderful
That you are to me
The apple of my eye
The desire of my heart
Unique and a 'one off'
Truly set apart
So don't look in this mirror
And critise what I've done
Your made in My image
My princess my called one

    Jesus

Each time Jesus looks at you
His heart flutters like
The beating of a butterflies wing

----------x----------

Faith - the constant belief and trust n the truth!

Have FAITH in God!

----------x----------

Take a moment now
To pull a funny face
Then have a laugh and thank the Lord
He's saved you by his grace

----------x----------

I'm not perfect yet but I'm in training! :)

----------x----------

Don't count the storms count the rainbows!

Unforgiveness is like carrying a rucksack of blocks on your back - it will weigh you down, distract you and even impact on your health. One by one let go and let God!

----------x----------

You need pruned in order to grow- don't despise Gods correction.

----------x----------

God paints a rainbow not with a brush but with His finger of mercy

----------x----------

Are you up for a challenge?

How dull life would be
If God made it all black and white.

Challenge for today :
Add colour to someone's life!

How?
A kind word, a smile a hug.
It doesn't take much, costs nothing and it's value is priceless.

----------x----------

Remember when the winds blow
And the waves are high
Jesus says "come"
You can walk on water
When you keep your eyes on Him

Rest is not something we work towards
Or strive to achieve
It's a free gift from God
We just have to receive

----------X----------

If you hold on to resentment you will never have contentment

----------X----------

One person can stand in a crowded church and still feel alone. Be that someone's comfort. Don't think - just do!

----------X----------

A moment given of your time to notice someone can be a moment an un-noticed person will treasure for a lifetime

----------X----------

A moment of your time can be a life changing moment for someone else

----------X----------

When you reapply your lipstick
Take a moment to remember
Its not what you put on your lips that is important
It's the words you allow to come out of them that counts

A soothing face mask
Helps restore the skin
But the word of God
Brings healing within

----------x----------

Take a moment to ponder over
All the things and people around you
That you may take for granted
Don't neglect to thank God
For the small things in life
Discover the gift God has placed in your life
Then pursue it and live it with enthusiasm

----------x----------

God takes the small insignificant things
And transforms them for His glory
Any life and any gift
In His hands becomes an awesome story

----------x----------

When you look in the mirror what do you see
Is it just a girl or an image of Me
For I live within you and I want you to shine
So others will know you are a child of mine
So as you apply the sparkle that makes your face glow
Remember let your life shine for me
So others may know

God

All the beauty you see around you
Cannot compare to the beauty God sees in you

----------x----------

Love like you will never get another chance
Live with excitement and expectation
Laugh until your sides hurt and tears of happiness wet your face
Love, live, laugh
Enjoy life to the max

----------x----------

Have you are burden you cannot share
Then take it to God and leave it there
For He understands everything you go through
No worry too small and nothing He cannot do

----------x----------

Try not to be ...
so busy doing that you cannot see
So busy talking that you cannot hear
So busy thinking can't you cannot notice
Carry each others burdens

Stoop down and reach out to those who are oppressed. Share their
burdens, and so complete Christ's law. (Galatians 6:2 MSG)

As you feel the soft summer rain
Fall gently upon your face
Remember God catches every tear
And dries your eyes with His grace

----------x----------

Grace - unmerited favour send from above
Reminding us daily of Gods unconditional love

----------x----------

When your day feels like it's going 100mph just praise God you are
burning calories

----------x----------

Ever thought you would like a facelift ? Quick, free solution- SMILE

Smiling
Makes
Imperfection
Lines
Evaporate

----------x----------

Sometimes its good to relax with the pals
Grab a coffee and cupcake and forget about the cals!

By yourself you're unprotected. With a friend you can face the worst. Can you round up
a third? A three-stranded rope isn't easily snapped. (Ecclesiastes 4:12 MSG)

----------x----------

Life continually changes like each season
And only God may know the reason
But in these times hold on to Gods hand
He will lead and direct you to what He has planned

----------x----------

Every season has a reason!

To everything there is a season, and a time for every matter or purpose
under heaven: (Ecclesiastes 3:1 AMP)

----------x----------

As you gaze in the mirror making sure all is in tact
Spend just a moment to think about God and reflect

SELAH!

When your going about your day in a wander
Just take hold of this thought spend time to ponder
That no one or nothing no matter what you do
Can compare to how much God loves and treasures you

----------x----------

Take just a moment to thank God above
For his unending mercy, compassion and love
Grace ever flowing, strength new each day
Patiently waiting to meet with us as we pray

----------x----------

A woman's heart is a treasure chest
Filled with irreplaceable jewels
Gems of priceless worth
Stored so deep that nothing
Can steal away from what she places there
Sealed with tenderness and forever
Locked with the key of love

----------x----------

Complicated?

Men think women are complicated
Actually they are the opposite
Desiring only the simple things in life
Time, patience, love,
Tenderness, acceptance,
Understanding, honesty
Craving the very things
that we often don't get
Educate the men you know
In what it is that women want!

Pain

P owerful platform that God can use

A s we make up our minds to choose

I n the midst of failure remember the words YOU CAN

N ever ending opportunities with the right choices and Gods plan

----------x----------

Hugs

H earts touching

U plifting strength

G esture of affection

S afe embrace

----------x----------

Trust - In every day in every way put your TRUST in God.

T otal dependence

R eliance and confidence

U tter belief and certainty

S afe and secure

T ender hope

Rainbow Colours

The colours of the rainbow in full array
Shine forth each different and vibrant
Yet compliment each other
So in life don't be afraid to stand out
Embrace bring unique
God has made us all individual
So find your true colour
And paint your world

----------x----------

I was designed by the master creator, handmade with the finest detail in
a mould made just for me. So am I special - I think so!

----------x----------

Random

Take a moment to make someone's day

You don't need to fast about it or to pray

Smile, say hello give a hug or a kiss

Those things aren't even likely

To be something you'll miss
A random thought of kindness

A sudden act spontaneously
The value of these little randoms

Only heaven may see

Today change the routine
Go out of your way
To bless someone
Think outside your own little world
Seek to be a blessing rather than to be blessed

----------x----------

Revels

People can be like a bag of revels
You never know what you will find
Some you may prefer than others
But there's something in a bag for everyone
Don't live your life complaining
That others don't suit your taste
And don't try to be what you are not
Enjoy being the flavour God made you

God will bring those to you who love who you are

----------x----------

God will make a way

When God has a plan and you hold his hand
Then it won't matter if people don't understand
For stumbling blocks may appear but come as they may
It can't stop what God has for you He'll make a way

----------x----------

As the wings of each beautiful butterfly
Display an array of colour
Unique to each and everyone
So too we are made in Gods image
And display the colour of God
We are created one of a kind for a reason
Let the vibrancy of your colour shine forth
Paint this world with the colour God made you
May we, as Gods creation,
Live life as He designed
Bringing glory to the Creator
Let your colour shine!

----------x----------

Life continually changes like each season
And only God may know the reason
But in these hard times hold on to Gods hand
He will lead and direct you to what he has planned

Every season has a reason!

To everything there is a season, and a time for every matter or purpose under heaven
(Ecclesiastes 3:!)

As you gaze in the mirror making sure all is in tact
Spend just a moment to think about God and reflect

SELAH

----------x-----------

When you're going about your day in a wander
Just take hold of this thought and ponder
That no one or nothing no matter what you do
Can compare to how much God loves and treasures you

----------x----------

Take just a moment to thank God above
For His unending mercy, compassion and love
Grace ever flowing, strength new each day
Patiently waiting to meet with us as we pray

Seasons

In this section you can find poems relating to seasons such as summer or Christmas or seasons in a persons life. We all go through many seasons but God is the constant in our lives and He never changes.

Mothers Day Poem

God designed and fashioned
A creation like no other
And when He saw what He had done
He smiled and called her 'Mother'
The angels stood and marvelled
As they watched her from above
At such outstanding workmanship
The Masters touch of love
He shaped and moulded her with the grace
Of an eloquent bird in flight
He added a twinkle to her eye
The kind you'd see on a starry night
He filled her heart with amazing warmth
Like the sunshine of a summers day
And breathed upon her a gentleness
A soft breeze that cause leaves to sway
He added music to her heart
Strings of joy and kindness beyond measure
With chords of meekness and patience
Like an orchestra bringing pleasure
He carved her hands with mercy
To touch the hurting that come her way
And took time to make her as He desired
Just like a potter and his clay
He clothed her with strength and endurance
So through the difficulties she could still climb
Like the mighty majestic mountains
That stand the test of time
He etched her face with beauty
And set compassion in her eyes
So she could see and feel
The pain when someone cries
He smoothed her skin with tenderness
Her touch would be so mild
That just one stroke of her finger
Would calm a sobbing child
He anointed her with wisdom
A mothers instinct she would say
Made stronger and more distinctive

Mothers Day Poem.......continued

Each time she would pray
He opened her ears to listen
And gave her a quiet voice like a calm, moonlit sea
Yet her passion and desire for her children
Would flow like a volcano unstoppable and fiery
He stretched His hand out towards her
Symbolic of what He wanted her to be
Filled with so many qualities and gifts
He said "on this earth be an extension of Me"
God created a mother
With a plan and purpose in mind
A calling only she could fulfil
Unique one of a kind
So now would be a good time
To hug a mother and remember to say
You are special, loved and appreciated
Have a wonderful, happy mothers day!

Easter

E xtravagant love beyond compare

A stonishing victory for all to share

S alvation provided sins washed away

T ruth - Jesus reigns and is alive today!

E xtraordinary mercy the battles been won

R esult- it is finished Jesus rules number one!

Seasons
(going through divorce)

Life is a continual change of seasons
As the daybreak of **SPRING**
Awakens out hearts
With newness and excitement
Our minds are fresh
And our pulse beats fast
Like the wings of a newly launched butterfly
As we become captured
With the beauty all around us
And the awe and wonder of new life
Right now all is well!
Then the sizzling **SUMMER** heat
Brings forth an array of colour
All that we see blossoms and grows
Reaching its full potential
Making our hearts skip for joy
Full of warmth and expectancy
Nothing can erase the smile
From a face in a beautiful summer season
Then along comes a cooler breeze
As **AUTUMN** slowly approaches
We gaze in amazement
At the display of changing colours
And don't notice so much
That the summer season has ended
Its not until we see the falling leaves
That we wonder - what happened?
Then what seems to be all of a sudden
We are thrust into a **WINTER** wonderland
Although beautiful and inspiring
Its cold and lonely
Bringing the need and longing for comfort
We look back wondering
Where did summer go?
I was happy then.
But remember every season lasts just for a time
Seasons can be difficult and enduring
But if you search you will find beauty in them all

Seasons

(going through divorce)........continued

If your heart feels heavy and sad
Like the dark clouds in the sky
And your heart leeks with disappointment
And thumps with pain
Like a mighty thunder storm
And you feel the sun will never shine through
And the day will never brighten
Remember spring is on its way
Bringing once again
Warmth, new beginnings and colour
Spring will change the black and white of winter
Into a rainbow of colour that will brighten your life
And bring you hope

Easter Story

Walking into that cold, damp room
He hears voices in a debate
"I'm the greatest" "it must be me"
"No it's me He said I was great"
With a heavy heart Jesus looked on
He watches them find a space for a seat
And with humility and grace He kneels down
With a cloth and basin to wash their feet
Now the voices that so frustratingly raged
Are silenced with this simple act
With heads now hung low they quietly observe
Taking this moment to gently reflect
With one simple sentence He reminds them all
"As I've served you now serve one another"
Hoping this moment will last them a lifetime
And this truth they will live out with no bother
He takes his place on the floor among them
His mind a battlefield knowing what's ahead
Yet with inward strength He tells them
"Take eat this is my body" as He breaks the bread
Then raising the cup He says "drink all of it
This is My blood shed for you"
As He knows the time is now close
For what His Father desires Him to do
They go to the garden of Gethsemene
He prays earnestly - Gods only son
"Can this cup pass from Me?
Yet not My will but Your will be done"
As He stands to His feet his disciples
Are wakened by the sound of clamouring armour and swords
Torches flicker in the distance
As the soldiers all come in one accord
Judas, with his silver, walks forward to greet Him
With a gentle kiss on the cheek
As the soldiers proceed to arrest Him
Saying "is this the Jesus we seek?"
And so His journey begins
The mockery, the torment the pain
As they strip Him and beat Him continuously

Easter Story.........continued

They whip Him and do not refrain
After some time He is sentenced
The people cry out "send Him to the cross"
They spit on Him, curse at Him and kick Him
Hurling insults and picking up stones to toss
Yet with dignity and compassion beyond measure
He climbs through the pain, up Calvarys hill
Where the sky turns black as night
And the world becomes silent and still
Mary His mother looks on heartbroken
Wishing she could be exchanged in His place
As her salty tears pour from her swollen eyes
Like little streams running over her face
In that hour as the sins of the world
Rest upon Him a heavy burden to bear
The crowd look to Him on the cross
Thinking "who is this that we've put up there?"
Then He finds one last burst of energy
And cries out with His final breath
"Father in heaven it is finished"
That moment marked history with His death
They placed His body in a tomb
The religious leaders thought that ended their grief
But to Jesus' followers their pain would soon turn
Into overwhelming joy and relief
As on the third day the tomb was empty
The stone had been miraculously rolled away
As Jesus appeared in the flesh
The disciples didn't know what to say
He sent them all out with the commission
To preach the good news and to share
The vast immense love of God
And how much for each of us He DOES care

Beautiful Day

The sun arises to announce the dawn of a new chapter
Filled with wonder and surprise
Its warm glow soothes the aches of cold sad days
Erasing them from our memory
The birds rejoice with a happy song
Excited as they bathe in the sun rays
Cooled by a gentle summer breeze
The long blades of lush green grass softly sway
Like a sail boat on a calm ocean sea
The powder blue sky is splashed with colour
Like a watery paint brush drawn across a blank page
The flowers open up with their vibrant colour
Together in unity they celebrate their creator
Perfuming the air with their fragrance
Alluring all that take time to notice
What a perfect God to create such a beautiful world!

Christmas Story

A little light flickered in a tiny room all night
And a soft, gentle voice
Whimpered " Joseph will we be alright?"
With a little reassurance she rested her head
While he knelt by the bedside
And all night he prayed
Then early that morning
They arose before the sun
Taking the little they had
Their journey now begun
She sat upon the donkey
The day would be long
While she quietly reminded
Herself to stay strong
The donkey grew weary
And the journey was so rough
Uneven pathways, bumpy roads, it was tough!
Her young, tiny frame
Bounced about – side to side
While she cradles her tummy
Protecting the new life inside
She looks at her husband
His feet blistered and sore
But he found the strength
To travel "just a little bit more"
Despite all her agony
She called herself blessed
And she thanked God above
He'd find her somewhere to rest
Hungry and weary they manage a grin
As they see in the distance, Bethlehem – there's an inn
Slowly they approach and knock on the door
Her eyes filled with tears
When she hears "room for no more"
And so they keep going
But the reply is the same
"No room at the inn
Sorry it's a shame"
Then finally an innkeeper

Christmas Story........continued

Greatly moved by what he saw
Said "you may stay in my stable
I'll make a bed with dry straw"
Grateful and thankful he helps her to the ground
They pause for a moment
And just look around
They cry out with thanksgiving
For Gods mercy and grace
For bringing them this far
And finding this place
Then all of a sudden
With great pain and despair
She cries out "it's the baby he's almost there"
They fix her a place to lie
The best that they can
How can this happen here
Is this all part of Gods plan
Minutes turn to hours
As she cried with the pain
She never felt such agony
Over and over again
Then finally the time comes
Joseph wipes her brow as everyone watches
Even pigs, lambs and the cow
The sound they've awaited
That cry brings such joy
In that muddy old stable
He kisses her – it's a boy!
His arrival is announced by a bright shining star
Resting above the stable it was seen from afar
Sounds like a lovely wee story
But the fact is its true
That Christ came from heaven to save me and you
Now that its Christmas
And life seems crazy and packed
Think of that stable and take time to reflect
In the joy surrounding Christmas
Wouldn't it be a shame if we didn't take time
To even mention His name

Christmas Chaos

Driving through the city on a chilly afternoon
Thinking I'd better hurry
The shops are closing soon
The Christmas lights are twinkling
And the carollers sing their song
No time now to stop though
I really haven't got that long
The cars are forming a massive queue
And the horns begin to beep
While the homeless man beside the bin curls up to go to sleep
Mobiles waving in the air
For reception to text or call
While little kids squeal with delight
As the snow begins to fall
A sea of human bodies
With arms full of turkey meat
Don't notice the drunkard on the road
Staggering as he tries to find his feet
People passing judgment as they run to and fro
At the young girls heading to the clubs
Leaving with others they don't know
Droves of people hit the shops like a hurricane in full swing
While tiny tearful eyes look through the windows
Knowing they wont receive a thing
How do we miss the obvious
When we prepare for Christmas day
The hurting go unnoticed and God doesn't have a say
How do we miss the very point of what its all about
We forget our Saviour as we nip in and out
We fail to help those most in need
As we complain about what we have to buy
We fill the atmosphere with groans as we unload each sigh
So maybe this year when you shop you'll rest for just a while
And take notice of someone who may be in need
A little time or just a smile
And as we celebrate Christs birth
And as He watches me and you
May we slow the Christmas chaos
And think "what would Jesus do?"

Autumn

The seasons changing I love it so
Autumn winds begin to blow
Whistling a love song through the trees
While people watch in wonder at the changing leaves
From lush green colour to red, yellow, brown
They dance with the wind until they've all fallen down
A crisp colourful carpet covers the ground
While children play stamping listening to the crunching sound
Animals search for food with care
Storing up for the winter they must prepare
Time for hats and scarves say goodbye summer sun
A new season to enjoy
Autumn has now begun

Summer

I love the smell of summer
The kind that takes your breath away
While watching the stalks of wheat
In the fields as they dance and sway
I listen as the birds chirp happily
United in their song
Harmonising with each other
Knowing this is where they belong
The sweet perfume of summer flowers
Such aroma fills the air
The beauty in creation
Reminds us that God is there
Take time to simply pause
Listen and look around
Appreciate what God has made
Each summer smell and sound

Summer Time

S oft and gentle summer breeze

U plifting pollen to make you sneeze

M iracles happen all around

M ake time to listen to the summer sound

E energetic kids squeal with delight

R eleasing in the air a colourful kite

T ime seems to stretch with brighter days

I nvolving deck chairs and hopefully sunrays

M en get to cooking on the BBQ

E njoy summer time no matter what you do

A Fathers Heart

They often stand up tall and proud
And also burp and fart
But we all know how much we love
And treasure a fathers heart
They enjoy and nurture us as we grow
And like to teach us things
An amazing and special part of life
Such joy a father brings
He'll keep you safe within his arms
And you'll know he's always there
Although he seems so big and strong
He can handle you with tender care
A fathers heart is a precious gift
That God designed and created
It's value cannot be measured
And It never can be outdated

Fathers Day

A strong shoulder
A tower of strength
A man of courage
Who would go any length
To protect his family
With love and with care
Someone to rely on
Who will always be there
A hero, a role model
A priceless treasure
A protector and provider
Special beyond measure
Crafted by God
Words cannot convey
How much you are loved
Happy Fathers Day!

Christmas

The winter wind whistles through the cold barren trees
The robin sings softly as she enjoys her berries
The snow falls from heaven like jewels in the sky
Twinkling, glistening, as the winter wonderland draws nigh
Children play happily full of expectation and cheer
Their eyes dance with excitement as Christmas is so near
The carollers' voices in sweet unity sing
Accompanied by the chimes of the church bells that ring
The frosty night air gives a nip to your nose
Friends snuggle tightly wrapped up in warm clothes
The smell of the turf on the fire burning bright
Brings a warm happy glow to the faces at night
The hustle and bustle fill the streets with activity
But have they forgotten the real Christmas – the Nativity
So many distractions cloud the true meaning and reason
Of what we should celebrate on this joyful season
We have all heard the story and it aint no fable
Of how a long time ago in a dark, damp, cold stable
A little baby boy was born sent from above
To seek and to save this lost world through love
From the beginning he knew what the Father had planned
But still in obedience he held out each hand
Taking our sickness, our sorrow and sin
And offering to us forgiveness and a true peace within
So as we enjoy Christmas and spread Christmas cheer
Lets remember the reason that we are all here
To thank God the Father for sending His Son
And to thank Jesus who came for all He has done

Grieving Hearts

This is where I found so much comfort though writing poetry in times of heartache and pain. May these word bring you comfort as they did for me.

Mama I See Heaven

Mama I see heaven and my body isn't strong
I'm trying but I don't think I can hold on very long
The lights look really pretty and I can hear some people sing
An angel said If I let go I can travel on his wing
Oh Mama I don't want to leave you if I go will you cry?
But I hear God now calling me saying it's time to fly
Mama do you know I love you and will you be ok?
I promise I'll look down on you and cuddle you each day
I'm sorry Mama I must go I'm weak now from the fight
God has promised He'll pour down love and you will be alright
Oh Mama now I'm flying it's so beautiful up here
I never will forget you I promise I'll be near
Don't you worry Mama I'm looking up into Gods face
His eyes are telling me it's ok He'll give you sufficient grace
Oh Mama I sure miss you but one day together we will be
Until then I'm playing with angels and sitting upon Gods knee

From your little angel

Never forgotten

I never saw you my little Angel
Or smelt your precious skin
I didn't even get a chance
To feel you kick within
I'll never see you grow up strong
Or play games in the park
Or comfort you at night time
If you were fretful in the dark
I didn't get to hold you tight
And safe in my embrace
Throughout my life I'll always wish
I could kiss your little face
What did you look like? A boy or girl?
Why did you have to go?
I guess I'll always have questions
With answers only God does know
I never got to touch or hold you
Or listen to your cry
Why did God choose so soon
To give you wings to fly?
You'll always be my baby
And although right now we are apart
The love we share will keep us together
Uniting both our hearts
You'll never be forgotten
Your memory will stay true
Ill always send hugs and kisses
Just between me and you

Mummy's Angel

Mummy don't you cry for me
Don't you be upset
I understand your aching heart
Because we never met
But I was given a special job
And God just could not wait
And what a welcome I received
When greeted at heavens gate
I got my wings now Mummy
And I can even fly
But how it makes my heart sad
When I look down and see you cry
I want to see you happy
But just now sad covers your face
But you would change if you just knew
How much I love this place
When the sky is dark look up
And you'll see that I'm alright
God said I'm His little twinkle star
That would shine in heaven bright
Oh Mummy it is not the end
It's only just the start
For I will always live with you
Deep down inside your heart
So don't you weep no more Mummy
We both will be just fine
I love you so much already
Cause I am yours and you are mine
And when it's your time Mummy
Don't worry I wont be late
I'll be standing with Jesus
Waiting for you at heavens gate

Little Star

Nestled in a little bundle
Safe inside my womb
There you latched on tightly
With no shortage of room
So small I couldn't feel you
Yet I knew that you were there
Each waking moment I spent thinking
Of the life that we would share
Every day brought new hopes and dreams
For your little life inside
I was so excited for you to grow
As I was bursting with pride
But I had no idea
That God had a different plan
And until the day we meet
I guess I'll never understand
For the life He placed within me
He then took to heaven above
He needed you to be with Him
A perfect angel filled with love
I didn't have you long enough
But what we had means so much to me
My precious little twinkle star
I'll love you eternally

Snowflake

I stand here amazed and silent
Watching the glistening white snow
Fall from heaven
It covers the earth like a baby's blanket
Soft and comforting
I feel the clean, crisp air flow through me
As I close my eyes
And take a long deep breath
I watch as the flakes all float
Like tiny feathers through the sky
Then I stretch out my arm and open my hand
Gazing in awe and wonder as this miracle
Changes before my very eyes
I see how the falling flakes
Turn to weeping water
As they know their time has come to an end
I long to reverse it all and change it back
To the beautiful creation it was
Then the sun appears
And quickly my magical moments disappear
My heart is heavy
Cause I know I can do nothing
Yet that is life
That is what makes it so special
Everything changes
Nothing stays the same
Miraculous moments like these
Are short yet never forgotten

All Around Me

When the sun rises with its warm soothing glow
I think of your love that comforted me in hard times
Your embracing arms that covered and protected me
When the wind gently blows through the trees
I hear you remind me of all the things you taught
Words of wisdom and courage to uplift me
As nature beautifully changes colour and shape
I reflect on your unchanging love and faithfulness
You helped me grow and stand firm no matter what
When the heavens open and raindrops fall
I imagine all the tears you shed for me
And the prayers that you prayed by your bedside
As the sparkling stars majestically shine in the night sky
I ponder over the years you spent
Teaching, leading and guiding me inspiring me to dream
And as each new day begins without fail
I know in my heart that your love, like time,
Will never change but is new every day
So as I look at the wonder of Gods creation
I am forever thankful and grateful
For you my mother and my friend

The Big Oak Tree

Your memory's like a big oak tree that's planted in my heart
And it has grew up tall and strong since we have been apart
It's gently taken care of by happy thoughts down through the years
And it always is well watered by my 'miss you daddy' tears
And it will be more beautiful as time slowly passes by
And I can look on and reflect without wondering or asking why
Because your memories are my comfort and when I think of that oak tree
I still can feel your big strong arms of love wrapped all round me
I know I cannot bring you back but your life cannot fade
Because you left such happiness unforgettable memories you made
You will always be my hero the worlds greatest you are to me
And I will always love you forever and eternity

For my Dad - I love and miss you

I Miss You

All the little things I took for granted
Now they matter so much
The sound of your voice, that cheerful smile
Your loving tender touch
The way that you could look at me
And brighten up my day
I knew also that behind the scenes
You would take the time to pray
Your words of wisdom and just being yourself
All the little things you would do
Are constant moments I cherish
The joys of knowing and loving you

Goodbye

Floods of tears have now fallen
Upon this little grave
Tears of mixed emotions
Though I'm trying to be brave
I'm hoping to ease the agony
I've bottled all these years
Letting go of all my pain
Facing all my fears
But it is proving difficult
To say the word 'goodbye'
For just the very thought of it
Causes my heart again to cry
I love you both intensely
That's why it hurts this way
But its not that I'll forget you
You'll both be with me every day
Its time now for me to let go
Of the past and all its pain
And allow my heart to heal
As I think of you with a smile again
Its just a new beginning
The next chapter a fresh start
I always will remember you both
You are imprinted on my heart
I hope now as I live my life
You will be proud of all I do
For I know for sure til the day I die
I will be proud of you

In memory of my parents who died two weeks apart

Like A Leaf

Life is like a leaf
That falls from a tree
Some drift gracefully
Floating gently to their place of rest
Others fall suddenly
Their journey taking no time at all
Some are caught up with the wind
Pulled in all directions
Their journey is rough
They may be battered and torn
But they survive the storm
And sooner or later they too must rest
No two leaves fall to the ground the same way
So to our lives are all different
We all live and then die
But the journeys in between are all unique
My life has been like a leaf in the wind
Storms have taken me in many directions
But the One who is in control of the storms
Holds me gently in His hand
I have nothing to fear
No matter how strong the gales blow
He will cushion my fall to the ground
And when that journey ends
He will take me to where my new life begins

Memories (Death of Friend)

The times we had together
Are the memories I hold dear
You make me smile when I think of you
As if you still were really here
I'll treasure every thought of you
Now we are apart
And keep a special place for you
Deep within my heart

----------x----------

I'm so glad I had you In my life
If even just for a short while
The good times we shared together
Still light me up and make me smile
Not many have a friendship
Like we did so close and true
And I will always be thankful
For an amazing friend - that's you!

----------x----------

We only had a few years
But they counted as the best
Each memory that I have of you
Let's me know how much I'm blessed

Don't Cry I'm Here

Don't stand upon my grave and cry
I just moved on I didn't die
Don't be upset remember I'm not there
If you look around I'm everywhere
I smile through the sunshine up above
As it shines down on you with my love
And if you are hurting or in pain
You can see my teardrops in the rain
You can hear me speak in the rustling leaves
And feel my embrace in the gentle breeze
And when you look and see daffodils grow
Remember that I love you so
I am the breath beneath birds in flight
I look down from the shining stars at night
I am with you in the winds that blow
You can see me sparkle in the glistening snow
So do not grieve I have not gone
It's just a new chapter I've only moved on
Although you may think we are far apart
I am closer to you than each beat of your heart
Don't be sad or hold in your pain
Put your trust in God and we'll meet again
Remember the words that I taught you each day
And I will be listening to you as you pray

For my Mum

In My Heart

Although my eyes cannot see you anymore
And each part of me is aching and sore
I know you have seen each tear I have cried
And you're standing closely here by my side
I feel you watching each move that I make
I know you can hear each breath that I take
And though this parting may have been all Gods plan
It comforts me to know you are holding His hand
Although God has called you we are never apart
Because you live on each day in my heart
I know I have no reason ever to fear
Cause wherever I am you will always be near
You are just like an eagle that's been released to fly
Soaring so happily above in the sky
Watching and guarding our lives from above
Protecting your children with your wings of love
I will never forget you cause as each day goes past
My love will grow stronger til we meet at last
The memories you left will always remain
Close to my heart til we meet again

Broken Hearted

I know that you can see me
And can feel my broken heart
But living here without you
Feels like I've been torn apart
I miss your words of comfort
That calmed my every fear
Those loving eyes that told me
Don't worry I'll be here
I long to see your smile again
That changed my every frown
And feel those arms of comfort
That picked me up when I was down
Those hands that touched my many times
And wiped away my tears
Someone with a special heart
And always listening ears
I'm missing you like crazy
But I know that you're ok
And at least I have assurance
I'll see you again someday

I Miss You Already

Lonely and heartbroken
Afraid of how I feel
Holding in my emotions
So my heart becomes like steel

Missing you like crazy
Knowing moments from now you're gone
Sitting beside you helpless
As your spirit just moves on

How can I live without you
My Mother and my friend
The one who knows me deeply
So theres no need to pretend

As your tightened grip weakens
And you rest now from this fight
I want to say that I love you
And don't worry I'll be alright

I know you will be watching
As you look from up above
And as each day goes by
I'll always have your love

Etched in my memory as my Mum passed away

The Daffodil

In a beautiful scented garden
With a gentle breeze so still
I stopped and gazed upon a flower
A bright yellow daffodil
The storms would beat upon it
But it battled with all its might
And as the rain would fall
It made each petal seem more bright
This little flower had got life tough
But never once complained
It held its head up high
And simply smiled each time it rained
The other flowers with drooping leaves
Would stand amazed at this sight
They wondered among themselves
Where this little flower got such fight
But then one day this little flower
That God had planned and made
Looked around and gently smiled
And then began to fade
So I wondered to myself
As I breathed a heavy sigh
How could something so wonderful
Simply fade away and die
Then God showed me it was time
This flower served its purpose well
The time had come for it to rest
Now with Him it would dwell
This flower dedicated each moment
Showing others how life's worthwhile
And even through the tough times
To hold your head up high and smile
God promised me He had this flower
Held tightly in His hand
With this life He was well pleased
Cause it had done all He had planned

In memory of how my Mum battled cancer so bravely

The Flower

As I sit here quietly
I gaze upon the beauty of a flower
I marvel at the thought
Of how something so wonderful
Was once a tiny seed
As it was nourished
It developed and grew
Until it reached the point
Where it is at now
The long green stems
Provide support and vitality
While the little buds
Are just bursting with life
As they begin to open
Their beauty is overwhelming
Each individual petal
Show such character and personality
Their beauty surpasses
Everything around about
They say so much
Although they speak not a word
Their fragrance is their smile
A perfume no man could create
As you look upon their eloquence
Their stillness portrays such peace
Then – after a while
They whither and fade
Yet how can something so wonderful
Just simply die
They have had their season
And served their purpose well
They must now make room
For those that are to follow

My mum and my family

You're Like The Wind

I cannot see the wind
But I can feel what it can do
And though you've gone from sight
The same applies to you
I feel the gentle breeze
As it brushes through my hair
And I know the wind embraces me
To let me know you're there
Sometimes the wind goes by me
Like a whisper in my ear
And each times this happens
I hear you say "don't worry I'm here"
I cant describe how much I miss you
But I know you feel my pain
And I'm sure you miss me too
I see your teardrops in the rain
I long for us to be together
There's so much I have to say
But I know I'll have to wait
To God calls me someday

Beautiful Snow

I'm standing outside watching in wonder
As glistening white jewels fall from the sky
I close my eyes and feel them
Soft and cold upon my face
They fall like tears from my eyes
As if to say they know how I feel
Where have they come from
I cannot see their beginning just their end
Then I look around and see them
Lie gently under my feet
At first it feels safe and comforting
I want to stay like this forever
Then as I walk around
I feel how crisp and slippery
They have now become
How have these tears turned to hardness of heart
Still I do not want to let go
I try my best to steady myself
Without any help
Then the sun appears
And soon this cold, frosty ice begins to melt
Slowly they start again
Turning to eatery tears
I watch in hope that this weeping
Will return to snow but it cannot
As the sun begins to warm me
It feels painful
I know this has to happen but it hurts
I want the snow to stay as snow
It was beautiful, comforting, loving
Why did it have to change
Now that it has gone
I find my beauty, comfort, love
From the One who made the snow

Beautiful Memories

I often go for country walks
And so many days I've cried
Wishing you were still with me
Right here by my side
I look at all the scenery
But it just reminds me more
Of all the lovely happy times
That we had shared before
And then a gentle breeze can blow
And with a still small voice I hear
"Keep your chin up and go on
I always will be near"
I have so many memories
That I cherish and I treasure
So many that I couldn't
Take the time to ever measure
I wish we still could be together
To laugh and love and share
But I know that you are safe now
In the Masters tender care
I will always love and miss you
Nothing can ever take that away
Your memory grows more beautiful
With every passing day

There I'll Be!

A gentle trickling stream
Flowing happily over rugged rocks
Creating a beautiful song
That can only be heard
With a quiet heart
There I'll be!

The air beneath a flock of birds
As they fly effortlessly in unison
Gracefully soaring high in the sky
Able to see the world below
From a whole new perspective
Look up – there I'll be!

A magnificent array of colours
As a rainbow is swept over the sky
A brushstroke of promise
Displaying such joy, excitement and beauty
The calm after the storm
Smile – there I'll be!

The warmth of the sun
As it shines down upon you
Nourishing and comforting
Its ray of light illuminating your path
Bringing hope and expectation
Surrounding you – there I'll be!

The soft, soothing droplets of summer rain
As they fall tenderly upon your face
And gently massage your heart
Angels in heaven weep
To comfort you in your moments of pain
Imagine- there I'll be!

The magical sound of laugher
As children play contentedly
And your smile brings warmth
Brightening up the dullest of days

There I'll Be!........continued

Don't cry – for in laughter
Remember – there I'll be!

Feel the strength of the wind
As it sweeps your hair from your face
Lifting leaves with invisible hands
Reminding you that even unseen things
Are still very much around
Feel it – there I'll be!

In stillness when all is quiet
And you sit alone and ponder over memories
With overwhelming emotion
Which feels like a raging storm inside you
That stillness will be my embrace
Enveloping you – there I'll be!

When you wake to a new day
And you feel clouds overshadow you
Take courage for the sun will break through
Each breath that you take remember
My everlasting love will never die
The air you breath – there I'll be

Touching God's heart

The following poems are prayers and reflections on my love for God and His heart towards us.

Jesus You Are

The colour in my black and white
The wind that blows beneath my kite
The miracle that gives a blind man sight
You are …

The harmony in my souls song
Endurance to keep going when the distance is long
Perseverance and courage when things go wrong
You are…

Hope to the hopeless in times of fear
Joy to the heartbroken when they need cheer
Friend to the friendless as You draw near
You are…

More beautiful than words could ever say
Beyond what my imagination can possibly convey
All I need and more each day
You are…

The Lion of Judah yet a gentle lamb
In the fiercest storm you are the calm
Perfect redemption THE Great I Am
You are…

Rest

In Your awesome presence
My heart will be at peace
All worries, cares and burdens
At this moment seem to cease
For all that occupies my mind
Through the hustle of each day
When we meet together
Like max they melt away
For you are my strength and refuge
My anchor in the raging sea
And I know that you will keep me safe
Just cause you love me

Where In This World?

Where in this world would I ever be
Without your love wrapped all around me
Protecting and guarding me when I'm unaware
Listening and comforting telling me that You care
Where in this world would I ever go
Without your Spirits guidance when I just don't know
Prompting and nudging me the right way
Being my help mate every day
Where in this world would I ever turn
When the storms of life have me in a churn
But close by Your side is where I'm safe from harm
Held gently but firmly in my Saviours arm
Who in this world can save me from sin
Instead of condemnation leave peace within
For only You Lord can satisfy
You wipe the tears that this world makes me cry
You alone are all my heart longs for
I will love and praise You forevermore

Fill Me

Fill this empty vessel
With your mercy grace and love
May your Holy Spirit meet me
And rest upon me like a dove
I'm hungry for your touch Lord
Come and quench this thirst
May Your anointing overwhelm me
Pour into me until I'm immersed
Consume me with your presence
My heart and hands I raise
Overflow my life with passion
As I live with your name to raise

Reaching To You

As the petals of a flower stretch
Extending towards the hot radiating sun
So my soul reaches to you Oh God.
Take my hand and wrap me
In the warmth of your love
Consuming me with your power
As I become transfixed
On your outstanding beauty
Envelop me in your presence
And never let me go

Under The Shadow

Under the shadow of Your wings
I find shelter for my soul
You're my stronghold, my protector
You're the One who is in control

Under the shadow of Your wings
I can gaze upon Your face
You're my refuge from the storm
You're my God – full of mercy and grace

Under the shadow of your wings
All my brokenness You mend
You're my strength, my comforter
You're my Saviour, my best friend

Under the shadow of Your wings
I feel Your Spirit like a dove
You're my joy, my peace, my all
And now I rest in Your great love

Dark Night

Through the darkest times of my life when fear is in the air
I look across the night sky and I know that you are there
Though the waves crash fierce upon the shore
And it's so dark I cannot see
You send the moon to illuminate a path you make a way for me
With jagged rocks on either side each step I fear to tread
But then I see the lighthouse shining
So I keep my eyes on you instead
In those lonely fearful times Lord help me walk with faith not fear
May I despite the circumstances
Feel your help and presence near
When I worship you with all that I have
All around me fades away
And I know you'll take me by the hand leading me to a brighter day

Jesus

Wrap Your presence around me
Like a safe and warm embrace
Cover me with Your arms of love
Shine down upon me grace
Sooth me with Your mercy
As only You can do
And listen as I whisper
Jesus I love You

Always Near

In my weakest moment
When the battles been too long
You uphold me with your love
You are my strength my song
When I am overwhelmed with fear
And held in chains needing release
You whisper gently to my heart
Breaking shackles and leaving peace
No matter how isolated I feel
I know I never walk alone
For you gave your life a sacrifice
So you could call me your own
Thank you Jesus for your love
That upholds and sets me free
Along this road you hold my hand
And never will leave me

Morning Decision

I open my eyes and its morning
The room is still dimly lit
As I lay here I think to myself
Today I can press on or quit.
So easy to feel wore down and faint
As I think is it really worth the fight
But something within me wont give up
A small voice says " it's gonna be alright."
So I get up wash my face and get ready
And decide there and then come what may
That I can accomplish each task
When I call out to God and pray
He gives me new strength every morning
As I take time to seek His face
And I know whatever the day brings
He will pour upon me sufficient grace
So with a spring in my step and a new hope
I am ready and equipped at the break of dawn
To juggle the needs must of the day
All fired up I say BRING IT ON!

Tender Heart

Lord be tender with this heart of mine
As I place it in Your hand
Its fragile and I'm trusting You
I know You understand
You are the great restorer
The master potter with the clay
Well take and mould me for Your glory
Purify me Lord I pray
I give my all to You now
In surrender I worship in this place
Fill me with Your power
Overwhelm me with Your grace

Gods Grace

Beyond what my mind can comprehend
Further than infinity it knows no end
Has no limits it will always extend
Gods grace
Free to all it doesn't cost
A lighthouse shining when my ship is lost
In my life is now embossed
Gods grace
Soft as a petal on a summer flower
Beautiful and radiant as a twinkling star
Loves and reaches you just where you are
Gods grace
No comparison can justify
The depth or meaning the reason why
To take our sins – suffer and die
GODS GRACE

Let Go And Let God

Sometimes I don't know
The answer doesn't seem clear
My pathway is cluttered and etched with fear
But in the midst of the blur
There's a still small voice telling me softly
I always have a choice
I can face it alone
With worry as my guide
Or I can leave it with God
And trust God He's by my side
If I loosen the grip
And let go of stress as Gods planned
Then that leaves me free to take hold of His hand
So then I can take courage
That no matter what comes my way
God is close by my side and will go with me all the way

Simple Days

Lord some days are simple
Nothing bad or particularly good
Things tick along beautifully
Just the way they should
Help me in these comfy days
To take nothing for granted
May I be a blessing to others
Like water poured over a seed that's planted
Help to appreciate
The unseen help and answered prayers
And may I reach out to others
Showing them that someone cares

Shelter

When I see the storm a comin
And the chill of fear surrounds
I lift my eyes to heaven
My soul searches for higher ground
For You alone Lord Jesus
Are my anchor in the sea
My safe comforting haven
Your strong arms shelter me
When I'm in that place with You
It doesn't matter come what may
I know my boat wont overturn
Even though I feel it sway
You are the captain of my ship
The journey feels surreal
My compass in the open sea
The wind within my sail

Photographers Prayer

Lord help me to capture a picture with flare
Each click of the button a smile I can share
Memories created beautifully unfold
No words needed yet a story is told
Help me to be ready each and every day
To keep a sharp focus so come what may
That I will be able to spring into action
So I pray I'll stay fit to avoid ending up in traction
Stretch my imagination so as I shout to others 'say cheese'
I will see beyond the obvious and a perfect picture I'll seize
Help me with technology so I can keep people updated
With awesome scenes from the world you've created

I Need You

As I sit here quietly
A thought comes to me today
I realise just how much I need You
In every single way
Theres nothing that I can achieve
Without the strength you give
For all that I am comes from You
Even the very breath to live
Thank You for Your mercy
And Your grace that so lavishly
Bestows upon me daily
Love that wraps around me

K.I.S.S

Don't try and complicate your life
Or so many great things you will miss
Strip back to the basics
Life's more enjoyable when you ...

K eep
I t
S uper
S imple

Have You Noticed?

The girl that cleans the toilets
With sweat upon her brow
The busy woman who takes time
To say ' come lets talk about it now'
The man behind the scenes
Who arrives early to set up
The woman who faithfully every week
Prepares to fill your tea cups
The shy girl who decorates with detail
That no one pays much attention to
The people running around working hard
To gracefully serve me and you
The dedicated team in unison
Who give so much in every way
That person that notices when things aren't right
And quietly says ' I'll pray'
These are the ones God notices
That He strategically puts in place
To show others how to live
With humility and grace

Tattered Heart

I saw a little tattered heart
With a colourful design
Decorated with strips of ribbon
And I thought 'that's just like mine'
It looked a little tender
Needing handled carefully
Then I heard God say 'that's what I do
When you give your heart to me
I take the wounded and battered
Remnants of your heart
And I fix it gracefully together
So it won't fall apart
I weave colours into your life
Others will look and see
That even though the tough times come
I heal and restore so beautifully
When you feel that life has stripped you bare
And troubles never seem to cease
Just place your heart in my hands
I will transform it into an art piece'

I Love You

My love is without limits or questions
My acceptance beyond human compare
My grace overflows like a never ending fountain
My all I am willing to share
I've mercy that's new every morning
Your mind just cannot comprehend
How much I actually love you
And want to be your closest friend
Already I've given my life
What else could I possibly do
To prove how important you are to me
To show how much I love you

Jesus

Lay It Down

My child come close and lay your head here upon my knee
Let me wrap you in My love that lasts eternally
Rest your fears and worries that burden your heart sore
Lay them down as leave them here and child be anxious no more
For have I not promised you
To be with you all the way
To hold your hand - to carry you I'm just a breath away
So even though you feel I'm distant, no longer by your side
I want to remind you I'm still here and I've caught the tears that you've cried
So come reach out in faith find peace from worries and fear
And know for sure no matter what you're not alone I'm always near!

Your Father

Come To Me

Come let me hold you safe in My embrace
Where I will protect you cover you with My grace
Come and draw close there is nothing to fear
Hold on to My hand feel my presence near
My arms are wide open to welcome you in
There is nothing between us I have cleansed you from sin
Don't stand at a distance or worship from afar
I'm longing to touch you come just as you are
Lift your head high I want us to meet
To fellowship together will you dwell at my feet?
So come now receive what I have to give
I'm wanting to bless you a great life to live
Oh my dear child I love you more than you know
Just rest in my presence and heaviness will go
I'm calling you now I'm waiting patiently
My table is ready will you dine with Me?

Jesus

Come

Come to Me when you are weary
I will make you strong
I will dry away the tears
And give you a brand new song
Lay your head upon Me
And rest in My embrace
Let Me fill you now with strength
Overflow you with My grace

Jesus

Rise Up

Rise up wounded soldier
Secure your armour back in place
Shake the dust from off your feet
And get back into the race
The fiery darts have knocked you down
And I have heard your cries
But lift your head and hold it high
Its time now to arise
You've been attacked on every side
And you're wore out from the fight
But when you're weak I'll make you strong
I'll fill you with My power and might
Don't be discouraged stand your ground
And fix your eyes on Me
Together we'll walk through the storms
To claim the victory
So when you're exhausted, tired and weak
From the battles you go through
Remember I'm always by your side
I never will leave you

Jesus

Are You Ready?

I'm ready to pour out My Spirit
On this dry and thirsty land
I'm ready to move in power
With My strong and mighty hand

As you offer up your worship
And surrender all you have to Me
The clouds are becoming fuller
Look up and you will see

Are you ready for the next level
Can you handle what I have to give
For it will require devotion
In how you think and live

Keep on giving Me your praises
Wholly surrendering to Me your all
And in just a little while
The rain is going to fall

Are you ready, are you willing
Do you really want My touch
For I desire to consume you
Do you want me – just how much?

God

Surrender

Just close your eyes and meditate
Don't allow time or routine to dictate
For here I am beckoning you to come
To be with Me My daughters and My sons
Don't think of words or things to say
Just let My Spirit melt the cares of today
For I want to touch and take away your pain
I long to make you whole again
Don't try to impress Me with a long fancy phrase
Just pour out your heart surrender all in praise
Don't look back or look around
For where you are is holy ground
Oh My children if only you knew
Just what I've planned for you to do
But too many words and thoughts block out My voice
You're head's filled with ideas and matters of choice
But if in surrender you will come near
And listen intently then you will hear
My voice gently speaking guiding you day and night
Reassuring you no matter what you will be alright
So come draw near spend time with me
And I will show you things that are yet to be

Jesus

I Feel Your Pain

My child please will you listen
To My voice and understand
You are like a tiny baby
Help gently in my hand

I feel the piercing heartaches
And I see the tears you've shed
I understand the agony
And the reasons why your heart has bled

I am touched by your emotions
And I'm here to help you through
Draw close to Me, hold My embrace
That's all you have to do

I'm here with open arms
I want you to share with Me your pain
And I will comfort you with peace
And restore your joy again

God

Trust in Me

Are you wearied down with burdens
And does your heavy heart feel sore
Have the storms of life knocked you down
And you can take no more?
Does the road ahead seem all uphill
And you're exhausted, tired and weak?
Well then take the time to listen
To your Heavenly Father speak:
" I know the way seems barren
And you can't always understand My plan
But trust in Me to lead you through
Just hold on to My hand
Don't struggle in your own strength
You'll never make it on your own
I've promised I'll be with you
I'll never leave you on your own
So when you face the mountain tops
With clouds on either side
Hold on to My promises
And I will be your guide
When you're feeling lost and scared
Don't worry it will be alright
Remember that My promised
Will be your rainbows in the night"

God

Mountain Climb

I know you're tired and weary
From the battles you've been through
But have I not been faithful
In all you've had to do
Its hard sometimes to understand
Why you have to crawl through dirt and dust
But to achieve great things in life
Then sacrifice is a must
The mountain path is tiring
And its difficult to climb
But if you'll only persevere
You'll see the top in My time
Your hands and feet are aching
As you've held on so tight
But don't loose heart keep going
Everything will be alright
For I've been with you all the way
I've known your every fear
I've felt your discouragement and agony
I have caught your every tear
But I know that you can make it
And along this climb you may
Come across some others
That you can help on the way
So keep the mountain top in sight
Don't stop too long to rest
For when you reach the highest point
You'll know for you I've wanted the best

God

Always Near

Oh my precious child I've walked with you
Through all life's brought your way
I've never once forsaken you
Or left you for one day
I've sheltered you when storms have come
And from the scorching heat
I've wept with you when you have felt
That life just had you beat
I've laughed with you and felt your joy
When all was going well
And I've picked you up when many times
You have tripped and fell
I've felt your pain as you sat crushed
Perplexed your heart has cried
But you have never been alone
Because I'm always by your side
I've watched as you've pushed everyone away
And that included Me
But I knew my love would keep you safe
As I waited patiently
I never said life would be easy
Or the sky would always be blue
But I've promised no matter what
That I'd always walk with you
So in your darkest lonely hour
When you're gripped with fear
Remember closer than your heartbeat
I am always here
So never feel you are on your own
Or that no one can understand
Because you are my precious treasure
And I will always hold your hand

God

In This Mirror

When you look in this mirror remember that your Heavenly Father says

You are beautiful!
You are precious!
You are mine!

When you look in the mirror
I want you to see
How beautiful, how wonderful
That you are to me
The apple of My eye
The desire of my heart
Unique and a 'one off'
Truly set apart
So don't look in this mirror
And criticise what I've done
You're made in My image
My princess My called one

Just The Way You Are!

I watch you in the morning as you stretch and open your eyes
Lying there contented before the thoughts turn into sighs
I smile as you fix you hair and silently complain it is a mess
Because all I see it a jeweled crown on the head of my princess
I see you apply make up to your face and hear the thoughts within your mind
As you try to search for fresh wrinkles which show the years you've left behind
I hear the raging battles that you seem to fight each day
How it is you want to look different and you'll try come what may
To live up to expectations and keep up with the trend
But let me reassure you My daughter and My friend
Upon that face I see the girl that I created and I planned
Carefully sculpted with detail like a pot in a potters hand
No mistakes were ever made there never was a flaw
I knew exactly how you would be I was delighted with what I saw
Don't allow the pressures of this world to put cracks within my vessel
Even though at times it may seem a real big wrestle
For I've made you one of a kind sealed with my love and grace
And every day I breath a kiss from heaven upon your face
No matter how you think you look to me you shine as my brightest star
And nothing will ever change the fact
That I LOVE YOU JUST THE WAY YOU ARE

God

Tender Care

He wraps his tender arms around me
Like the wings of a gentle dove
And pours upon me grace
Surrounding me with a blanket of love
Throughout the raging voices
He whispers so softly and still
"My princess I'm right by your side
I'll protect you now and always will
So rest here in my presence
Let me care for you tenderly
For you're my little lamb
That I will love eternally"

I'm Here For You

My beautiful princess
You're right where you belong
I can feel your pain
As you sing to me your love song
You're here for a purpose
I want to whisper to your heart
As we draw close and embrace
Know you have a very special part
Rest in My arms I'll catch you as you fall
Realise I am proud of you
Rise up and stand tall
You are never alone
I'm right here by your side
If you were the only person on earth
I still would have died
No matter what you face
I'm here to take you through
Why? Well my gorgeous
Just because I love you!

God

Beautiful Princess

My sweetheart My princess My beautiful one
I've loved you and known you from before time begun
You shine like a star in the darkest of night
Your smile radiates so amazing and bright
You're created for now with a purpose and plan
Sculpted to perfection with My designer hand
So live out with passion what I've placed in you
Stand strong and courageous in all that you do
Be your sisters keeper no matter what it may seem
There is power in unity strength in a team

God

In The Hard Times

I know there are times
When quietly you feel lonely
A million questions in your mind
That end with 'if only' but please realise
I placed you right where you are
This bud will grow where others cannot
And will bloom into flower
Don't despise the tough times
Or where right now you may be
You are positioned for a purpose
So that others may see
That I am the Creator of heaven and earth
And position cannot measure
A persons value or worth
So just rest in Me now
Know your life's in My hands
You'll blossom in the hard places
Because it's part of My plans

God

Worshipping Heart in Song

This next section are some expressions of worship as I sat at the piano in my quiet time with God. My prayer is they will minister to your heart as you read.

Strength

Quietly she lay so still upon her bed
Tears ran down her face
As her hands they clutched her head

She looks towards the window
And sees a shooting star
Then I hear her bitter anguish
"Oh Lord you seem so far"

Gently she curls up so tired from the fight
Her relentless thoughts
Give her no rest in the night
Then I see her raise her hand
As she falls onto her knees
With a whisper I now hear
"Oh save me Jesus please"

Breaking through the silence I hear a soft voice gently
"You're not alone My child
I am just a breath away"
Then she casts her eyes to heaven
Letting go with a heavy sigh
And I hear Him gently tell her
"I will dry the tears you cry"

Lost in peaceful dreams she lies so very still
Enveloped with Gods grace
As He whispers to her His will
She will wake to face tomorrow
But now she's found a way
To ask and receive from God
The strength she will need each day

He gives strength to us each day
As we come to Him and pray
He gives strength

I See You

I see you, I see the real you
Though you try to hide
I stand here by your side
I see you

I see you, I see the real you
Take the mask from your face
I wait here with My grace
I see you

Let Me take you by the hand
Show you just what I have planned
Let all pretences go
I love you oh don't you know
That I see you
I see the real you

     Jesus

Grace and Mercy

Grace covers me
Like a blanket from heaven
It pours over me
Like oil from above
Grace covers me
Overflowing overwhelming me
With passion it envelops me
With my Fathers love

His mercy it pursues me
And reaches deep within
Bringing comfort and forgiveness
Cleansing me from sin
Oh grace and mercy
Follow me each day
And I'm forever thankful
I can live no other way

I Need You

Father wont You sit with me
Wont you bring peace to my soul
For I need You desperately
In my life to take control

For its only in Your presence
That I find strength for each day
Here I am now weak and weary
Saying come and have your way

Father wont You touch me now
With your mercy and your grace
Lift me in Your arms I pray
Hold me tight in your embrace

You Are My God

Jesus you are my God
My refuge in troubled times
My anchor through the storm
Jesus you are my God
My shelter my comforter
The arms that keep me warm

And so I lay it down to you
Each hope and each desire
Surrender and devotion
Is what you do require
You are my God, you are my God
You are my God

Father I Surrender

Father I surrender
As I fall upon my knees
Come now in this moment
Have your way within me please
I offer all I have to you
Though it doesn't seem that much
But I know that you work miracles
It only takes one touch

So I give myself completely
I place my all within your hands
Shape and mould me for your glory
Fulfill in me what you have planned

Eyes To Heaven

Though the cold north wind is blowing
And the Irish sea begins to roar
I will lift my eyes up to heaven
He will guide me through every raging war

Though the storms of life may come against me
And the rain beats hard upon my face
Still I lift my eyes up to heaven
For me strengthens me with love and grace

He's my anchor in the fiercest gale
He's my shelter, my refuge, place of calm
He is everything I will ever need
He's my saviour, my Lord the great I AM
He's my saviour, my Lord the great I AM

Whisper Over You

I whisper from heaven child
Words of comfort and words of grace
I sing love songs over you
Can you feel Me here in this place

For you are my treasure
My diamond shining bright
Through the storms you battle
Never give up in the fight
When you can't see the sunshine
I am here to help you through
My child – I am smiling over you!

        God

Consumed

On bended knee I come
Humbly now before you
Crying out to feel your presence near
Upon your alter I wait, I lay it all before you
With arms outstretched I come with reverent fear

So may your hand of mercy
Cover me as I desire
To be purified and cleansed
Consume me with your holy fire

Forgetting what's behind
I'm right here in this moment
In awe as you reveal yourself in this place
I feel your hand in mine
As you raise me to my feet
I know that I am covered by your grace

So may your hand of mercy cover me as I desire
To be purified and cleansed
Consume me with your holy fire

Lost

Lost within your love
Surrounded by your grace
Captured with your presence
Overcome now in this place
Oh breath upon me now
Holy Spirit touch renew
Closer deeper more
Overwhelm me Lord
with you

I Cry Out

Your spirit hovers over me
Like the mist on a mountain top
My heart cries out declaring praise
I yearn for you and cannot stop
I'm overwhelmed by your majestic power
Yet comforted by your gentle touch
Like a trickling stream over rugged rocks
You refresh my soul so much
All within me now surrenders
As a love song to you I sing
For I can hear you stir in me
A great awakening!

Abba Father Daddy

Abba Father , Daddy
I come before your throne
I'm thankful that you love me
And you call me your own

For my heart cries out in praise to you
I come on bended knee
Just to tell you that I love you
Abba Father my Daddy

Abba Father, Daddy
You surround me with your grace
Oh come reveal yourself to me
Let your presence fill this place

For my heart cries out in praise to you
I come on bended knee
Just to tell you that I love you
Abba Father my Daddy

Abba Father, Daddy
Before you now I fall
In worship and surrender
I give to you my all

In The Stillness

In the stillness of my soul
I lay down at your feet
Surrendered at your alter
I've come so we can meet
Take me consume me
Overwhelm me with your grace
Surround me with your presence
Come arrest me in this place
In the stillness of my soul
Oh Father hear my plea
Let me be lost in you
This is where I want to be

Beautiful

Beautiful You are beautiful
As I stand here in your presence
Nowhere else I'd rather be
Singing Father God I love you
You are beautiful to me

Wonderful you are wonderful
Your love and grace abounding
I can feel you breath on me
As I worship hear my heart cry
You are wonderful to me

Holy Spirit

Holy Spirit we cry come
Fill this room with your love and grace
We bow in adoration
Move among us oh come fill this place

On our knees we cry come Holy Spirit come
Touch us now breath upon us renew
On our knees we cry come Holy Spirit come
As we offer our worship Lord to You

Jesus - My Beacon In The Night

Jesus -my beacon in the night
My anchor in the storm
To you I'm holding tight
Jesus - the satisfaction I desire
You're all I'll ever need
Come set this heart on fire

To you I lift my voice my hands
In praise to you right now I stand
Come receive my offering
As I give my all my everything

Jesus - you fill my life and more
You have never let me down
You are worth living for
Jesus - here I am before you now
Humbly on my knees I cry
Touch me as my head I bow

To you I lift my voice my hands
In praise to you right now I stand
Come receive my offering
As I give to you my everything

Silent King

Silently a miracle was born
No fanfare, no trumpet or loud horn
Humbly in a manger there He lay
Sent by God to take our sins away

He didn't get the welcome of a King
Even though He was Lord of everything
But He came as a babe to earth for me
To give me life with Him eternally

So I now give thanks to Him in praise
As my voice, my heart, my hands I raise
I stand reflecting in this season
And I'm glad I know Jesus is the reason

I know that You came from above
A symbol of the Fathers love
And on a cross you cried "it's done"
Because of you are hearts are one

Butterfly Kisses

Some days I feel empty - lost in this place
Not sure who I am or who hides in this face
Then I cry out to God and I know that He hears
And despite how I feel he consoles all my fears

He sends butterfly kisses
To greet me at sunrise
So soft and so gentle
He wipes tears from my eyes
And all through the day
Amidst chaos and debris
He sends butterfly kisses
And I know GOD LOVES ME!

Life can be tainted by circumstances and choice
And somehow I struggle
To find my identity and voice
But underneath every trial
God waits patiently
Whispering " just let me love you
You belong to me"

So lift your head to heaven
Feel the wind of Gods grace
And let butterfly kisses
Fall upon your face

MY NOTES

MY NOTES

Lightning Source UK Ltd.
Milton Keynes UK
UKOW05f2127300813

216292UK00002B/6/P